MODERN SOUTHWEST COOKING

RYAN CLARK

RIO NUEVO PUBLISHERS

Tucson, Arizona

Rio Nuevo Publishers®
P.O. Box 5250, Tucson, Arizona 85703-0250
520-623-9558, www.rionuevo.com

The recipes contained in this book are to be followed exactly as written. Neither the publisher nor the author is responsible for your specific health or allergy needs that may require medical supervision, or for any adverse reactions to the recipes contained in this book.

Editor: Marilyn Noble
Design: Jamison Spittler, Jamison Design
Cover Design: David Jenney
Cover photos: Ryan Clark: Jill Schneider, Jill Photo; scallop: W. Ross Humphreys

Printed in Korea

10 9   8   7   6   5   4   3   2   1

Library of Congress Cataloging-in-Publication Data

Clark, Ryan, 1985–
  Modern Southwest cooking / Ryan Clark.
      pages cm
  ISBN 978-1-933855-91-2 — ISBN 1-933855-91-6
1. Cooking, American—Southwestern style. 2. Cooking—Arizona. I. Title.
  TX715.2.S69C55 2013
    641.5976—dc23   2013033317

Contents

INTRODUCTION

My Story. I always knew that someday I would become a cook—a good cook at that. Maybe even a chef. I did in fact become a chef, but I haven't stopped being a cook. By this, I mean I've never stopped working hard, never stopped learning, and never stopped eating.

I began my career in the epicenter of Southwestern cuisine at Chef Alan Zeman's restaurant, ¡Fuego! I quickly learned what it takes to become a chef and the lifestyle that engulfs you. The everyday life of a chef can be grueling, with long hours, hot kitchens, sharp knives, and punishing hangovers. But if you ask most chefs who are in it for the long haul they wouldn't change a thing. After my experience at ¡Fuego! I decided to enroll in culinary school. I figured I would get only one shot at a fundamental education, and so, at the age of twenty, I decided to take the scholarships I'd earned and put them to use at The Culinary Institute of America (CIA) in Hyde Park, New York.

Culinary school was a life changer. The diversity of people, strict schedules, levels of professionalism, and my colleagues' alarming passion for all things culinary were eye-openers for a Tucson boy.

The CIA program is built around a military structure. This means strict guidelines: clean-shaven every morning, pressed coat and slacks, polished chef shoes, and punctuality. On occasion, the instructors would even smell our breath before class, first to see if we had brushed our teeth, and second, to see if we had been out drinking the night before. It wasn't easy, but after three years of hard work and determination, I graduated from CIA with Dean's List honors. During my time at CIA, I was a finalist for San Pellegrino's Almost Famous Chef Award two years in a row and was named one of the top 16 junior chefs in the United States by the American Culinary Foundation. But even more important than the honors, CIA had developed in me the skills and passion for being a chef.

After finishing my culinary degree, I took an internship at Elements at the Sanctuary in Paradise Valley, Arizona. I worked alongside some amazing chefs, including Executive Chef Beau Macmillan, a Food Network Iron Chef and food celebrity. The culinary scene at the time had put Elements on the map as a celebrity hot spot. It gave me the opportunity to cook for such personalities as Wayne Gretzky, Britney Spears, Will Smith, and Sting.

My 18-month internship went faster than I had expected, and despite an offer to stay at Elements, I returned to my roots and moved home to Tucson. I took a job at Canyon Ranch, one of the country's premier health resorts, as a supervisor and butcher. It was a comfortable job because I was able to work by myself and at my own pace. I called it a scratch butchery because I would receive fresh seafood and meat orders daily and then fillet whole fish, grind fresh meat, and naturally cure special cuts. We sourced only organic, grass-fed, and sustainable products, and they were the best I had ever seen in any restaurant where I had worked or volunteered.

The next year, a great opportunity opened up for me at The Dish Bistro, a Tucson favorite. Owner Tom Smith and Chef Martin Swindells allowed me to join their team as *sous* chef. The scratch kitchen, seasonal menu, and small-plate dining experience changed the way I viewed food. My drive for using sustainable products and my relationships with local purveyors grew over my time at The Dish.

One day I received a call from Alan Zeman, the ¡Fuego! chef I had worked for years before. He told me to check out the chef opportunity open at Lodge on the Desert. So I did. The resort had been around for 71 years when I applied, although I had never heard of it. No one else I knew had heard of it either. Now, years later, we've created a name for Lodge on the Desert as one of Tucson's renowned dining experiences: three-time Tucson Iron Chef, The People's Choice Best New Chef nomination from *Food & Wine* magazine, World's Greatest Margarita at the Seventh Annual World Margarita Championship, and top accolades on tripadvisor.com and opentable.com.

So that's my story. I've left out the burnt steaks, profanity, and long nights of drinking with my fellow chefs, but I'm saving that for another time. I hope you enjoy my food and this collection of recipes showcasing my unique style of cuisine.

It's Okay to Play with Your Food

My culinary background is traditional. I trained at a school focused on French cuisine where students don't get A's for showing off and would certainly be put in detention for most of the dishes in this book. But I always like to try new things at least once, and I hope you do, too. Some of the techniques in this book may seem different and maybe even a bit intimidating, but really they are simple and proper. I say "simple" because, in most cases, the tools will do all of the work for you and make you look like an expert. And "proper" because most of the techniques I share with you are literally the proper and best way to do things. Over the years, I've played with many different cooking techniques, and these are the ones that, in my experience, work best.

The days of traditionalist food are over. It's time to play with your food, and I don't mean shaping your mashed potatoes into Mount Rushmore. We're talking about playing with textures, flavors, colors, and tastes, creating culinary surprises that shock all of your senses. Let's sprinkle some bacon-scented powder on your popcorn, and then, when it hits your tongue and melts into that unctuous goodness, you realize—it *is* bacon. Your friends will think you spent all afternoon simmering that thick, rich sauce, but really, all it took was a little pinch of agar-agar or xanthan gum. Have you ever experienced whipped dessert curd with a fresh scallop? Or a cocktail that tingles in your mouth with carbonated fruits? How about making ice cream in seconds, right in front of your guests?

We'll keep things simple and, most important, make sure everything tastes and looks delicious as we play with our food.

The Chef's Toy Box
We're not talking about dolls and G.I. Joes. These are the chef's tools of the trade, and it all starts with the basics.

Chef knife First, the chef knife. It needs a comfortable handle and balance that feels right to you, along with a style that fits not only your  needs, but maybe even your fashion sense. Your chef knife should be durable and well made. It's important to care for your knife like you would any other prized possession. I've had the same chef knife for 12 years because I take care of it. This means hand washing, daily honing, the occasional sharpening, and safe storage. Spend the bulk of your budget on one great chef knife. Yeah, it's nice to have a fillet knife, tomato knife, bread knife, slicer, and so on, but what's the point if they all suck? Spend your bucks on a good knife.

Wooden spoon Having a well-made wooden spoon makes all the difference when you're making sauces or need to get into the little curves of a pot of molten burnt sugar caramel. I'll be buried with my chef knife, but my wooden spoon I'll pass down to my children.

Spatula In case you were wondering, it's not your spatula that makes food stick to the pan, it's you. But it doesn't hurt to have a good one in your toy box. I carry two. A trusty fish spatula is a must. For the little jobs, I use a three- to four-inch offset spatula. One of these will keep you out

of trouble when it's time to plate up the beautiful rhubarb chiffon cake that you might just drop on the floor if you try to use a butter knife.

Timer No chef is perfect, and from time to time we forget time. A timer is key to running an efficient and functioning kitchen. It will pay for itself the first time it reminds you to pull a 60-dollar pan of curried pecans from the oven before they burn to a crisp. So splurge and get the timer with a digital probe. This will allow you to roast meats to the perfect temperature while still being able to keep time for those precious brandy snaps.

Turning slicer and mandoline And what about the fancy garnishes and perfectly sliced veggies? It's time to toss out the garlic press and pineapple corer to make room for a Benriner turning slicer and Benriner Japanese mandoline. These tools will help you achieve perfect julienned vegetables and even turn fresh yams or sweet potatoes into pasta noodles. Don't forget to use a pair of cut-proof gloves with these bad boys. There's too much food to be cooked for you to lose a finger. Seriously.

Tongs So, how do chefs get those pretty plates assembled so perfectly? Practice. Oh yeah, and some nice tongs. Every chef uses a different pair of tongs. I carry two in my toolbox. It's important to have a sturdy pair that can help sauté, grill, and remove a pan from the flames. But plating an exceptional dish in front of your guests always looks better when you use a petite pair of forceps, rather than your kitchen-beaten hands.

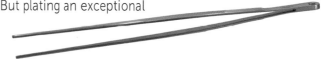

Besides, using a precise pair of tongs to place those tiny garnishes of micro sea beans and puffed rice just seems right.

Pots and pans None of these tools matter if you don't have the proper pots and pans. I go by the same rule I applied when I bought my truck: the heavier, the better. You want a thick, heavy bottom that will disperse the heat evenly and keep you from burning foods. You need a sturdy handle—one that's oven-proof so you can move from the stovetop to the oven to finish cooking that pan-roasted squab. But don't get

crazy. Unless you're opening up the next trendy, 10-item, happy hour spot, you should need only a saucepot, large and small sauté pans, and a 6- to 8-quart stockpot. I also like to have a non-stick pan for eggs.

You'll be meeting several nontraditional home-cooking techniques throughout this book, and I would like you to shake hands with them first while I do the introductions so you're not intimidated later on.

Sous vide system The age of your mom's ceramic slow cooker is over. Please welcome the *sous vide* process to your home kitchen. So what is *sous vide* and what makes it worth the investment? *Sous vide* simply means "under vacuum," and that's the first step. After seasoning or marinating a food item, whether carrots, filet mignon, or eggs, you vacuum seal it into a plastic bag and cook it in a water bath at a precise temperature for several hours. The result is food cooked perfectly. *Sous vide* allows us to control the cooking environment—the seasonings that go into the food before cooking, the flavor and nutrition during cooking, and the level of doneness at the end. Meat cooked *sous vide* will be consistent from the outside throughout the entire cut. Finally, you can cook the perfect medium-rare steak without any worries.

To cook *sous vide*, you'll need a vacuum sealer and a self-contained water bath oven or an immersion circulator and a large pot. You can find a *sous vide* system at most kitchen stores or online, and while the price tag is what you might consider a culinary investment, you'll probably find yourself using it all the time, especially because you can set it and walk away.

If you don't have a *sous vide* appliance handy and aren't exactly sold on spending big bucks on this gem, then try this: Place a kitchen towel in the bottom of a six-to-eight-quart stockpot and then fill it with

water. Attach a digital thermometer. The thermometer will measure the temperature of the water, and the towel will give you a bit of an insulation buffer from the direct heat from your stove top. Heat the pot and, when it reaches the desired temperature, adjust the burner to maintain it. Have some ice cubes handy in case you get the water too hot and need to cool it quickly. It's important to keep the temperature consistent, as a variation of even a half-degree can dramatically change the cooking time. It may take some babysitting to get the best results from your do-it-yourself food Jacuzzi. After doing this a couple of times, you may decide it's worth the bucks to buy the appliance.

Cream whipper For old-fashioned sodas, carbonated fruits, warm foamed sauces, and instant infusions, cream whipper canisters are a must. Simple recipes can become more complex and further detailed with the simple addition of carbonation. I like to use the smaller half-liter models that fit easily in a drawer and require fewer CO_2 charges than a normal size.

Handheld smoker Adding and layering flavors sets you apart from other cooks and their recipes. The Smoking Gun is a handheld smoker that allows you to add a smoky flavor to almost anything, including herbs, butter, and raw seafood. Place a small amount of wood chips into its vacuum—I like to use different teas and even bitter wood, but the traditional hickory or mesquite will do just fine—light the chips, and then the vacuum will pull oxygen through it and expel the smoke. The advantage of using this tool is that you're not adding heat along with the smoke. So you can explore smoking fruits and vegetables or even cocktails.

Key Ingredients

Creating something to eat always starts with conceptualization, just like the recipes in this book. But before we get to that point, we have to source ingredients.

It is important to understand that every ingredient is a key ingredient and should be treated as such. Just because onion is a supporting ingredient in a recipe doesn't mean that onion shouldn't be special. It should be fresh, local if possible, cared for and stored correctly, and organically and sustainably grown. Have fun with this cookbook and play with the recipes based on what you find at the market. If fresh shrimp aren't available, go for the diver scallops. Adjust the recipe to make it work. Chefs do this every day, whether cooking *à la minute* (prepared to order) or during seasonal menu planning. Looking at every ingredient in this way changes how we view food and put together recipes.

Every piece of produce is different. They speak to us in different ways and encourage us to cook them at certain times. If you're unsure about what's local and in season, go to the farmers market. See firsthand what's available. The farmers will be happy to talk to you about what's fresh and how to spot it. And, more important, they'll tell you what they'll have available in the coming weeks. Look toward the future and be the first to grab the squash blossoms for your next dinner party. Or get your hands on fresh goat cheese during the spring when it's richer and creamier than at any other time of year.

Remember, every ingredient is a key ingredient.

HYDRATION AND LIBATION

Drinking would fill up a pie chart of activities for most chefs. Not just the 2 a.m. kind, but the it's-hot-in-here kind and the let's-go-another-eight-hour-shift kind. Every place I've worked, chefs have had their go-to beverage during service. The skinny chef (whom no one trusts) drinks water from a deli container. Then there's the prep chef who drinks soda like it's going out of style. And there's always the one who brings in the two-for-$5 Red Bulls. Kitchens are hot. I mean 120 degrees on the line, cook-you-to-a-nice-rare hot. In this section, the first beverage, *juego,* is one we make in the kitchen to hydrate and keep the chefs from boiling over. And after a twelve-hour, strenuous workday spent climbing out of the weeds, we end this section with a stiff Chef's Manhattan. Cheers.

Juego

✓ ## Juego Makes 3½ quarts

As the kitchen gears up for the evening service, the chefs take a break and then prepare to get "stuck-in" on their stations. It will be five solid hours of standing over flames and enduring constant blasts of heat. The prep cooks prepare a batch of this prior to service to keep us all hydrated, cool, and pushing through the flames.

2½ quarts filtered water

¼ cup ~~agave syrup~~ *maple syrup*

~~1 teaspoon salt~~

3 oranges, juiced

2 lemons, juiced

1 lime, juiced

In a 1-gallon serving pitcher, mix the water, agave syrup, and salt until dissolved. Add the orange, lemon, and lime juices to the pitcher and stir well. Add ice and serve.

Campfire Serves 2

This cocktail reminds me of sitting on the lake in a summer breeze, not just because of the obvious smokiness of the drink, but also because you'll never find me vacationing on the lake without some tequila. You can easily find smoked salt online, but if you're adventurous enough to make it yourself, try setting a pan of kosher salt in the smoker the next time you fire it up for an overnight brisket or pork butt.

1 tablespoon smoked sea salt

½ cup grapefruit juice

2 shots silver tequila

1 shot triple sec

¼ cup citrus syrup (recipe follows)

2 grapefruit twists for garnish

Prepare two rocks glasses by moistening the rims with water or grapefruit juice and dipping them into the smoked sea salt. Fill a mixing glass or shaker with large ice cubes.

Add the grapefruit juice, tequila, triple sec, and citrus syrup and shake well. Strain into the prepared glasses with fresh ice and garnish with a grapefruit twist.

Citrus Syrup Makes 1 cup

No excuses for not having this sweet-and-sour bartender staple in your fridge. Replace the pre-made junk and go fresh.

½ cup freshly squeezed lemon juice

¼ cup freshly squeezed lime juice

⅓ cup sugar

Place the lemon and lime juices and sugar in a small saucepan and bring to a boil over medium heat. Stir until the sugar is melted and remove from heat. Cool completely and store in a clean juice jar or airtight container for 3 days.

Simple Syrup Makes 1½ cups

This is such a simple thing to make (hence the name), and it's good to have on hand for tea, coffee, and those occasional mixed cocktails.

1 cup sugar

1 cup water

Combine the sugar and water in a small saucepan and bring to a boil over medium heat. Stir until the sugar is dissolved. Remove from heat and cool completely.

Store in an airtight glass container in the refrigerator for up to 3 days.

Ginger Syrup Makes 1½ cups

Sweet and a bit spicy, this simple syrup can sweeten up any drink, from iced tea to lemon drops.

1 cup sugar

1 cup water

1 ounce fresh ginger, peeled and sliced

In a small pot over medium heat, mix the sugar, water, and ginger. Bring to a simmer and cook until the sugar is dissolved. Remove from heat, cool, puree, and strain. Store in a tightly sealed glass jar in the refrigerator for up to one week.

Cherry Cola Serves 2

This is a grown-up version of a kid drink. Use good bourbon and focus on the cherries. All-natural maraschino cherries without the artificial colors and preservatives are a must. Now that you have these two ingredients conquered, you have to choose a cola, but don't spend too much time—it's only a splash.

10 natural maraschino cherries

4 ounces Blanton's bourbon
(or your favorite)

2 tablespoons cherry juice

2 tablespoons fresh lime juice

¼ cup ginger syrup (recipe page 12)

2–3 dashes cherry bitters

light splash of cola

2 lime twists

Muddle the cherries in a mixing glass or shaker.

Add the bourbon, cherry juice, lime juice, ginger syrup, and bitters. Add ice and shake well.

Strain into two rocks glasses filled with ice, top with a splash of cola, and drop in a lime twist.

Sparkling Agua de Jamaica Makes 2 quarts

You can find this drink just about anywhere in the Southwest. Also known as red juice, it's the simple, decaffeinated alternative to iced tea. Step it up a bit with some sparkling shiraz, if you like. A few bubbles never hurt anyone, right?

1 pint water

½ cup sugar

½ cup dried hibiscus flowers

2 limes, halved and juiced

1 (750-ml) bottle sparkling shiraz
or other sparkling wine

Heat the water and sugar over medium heat in a saucepot. Once the sugar is dissolved, remove from heat, add the hibiscus flowers, and let steep for 5 minutes.

Strain and pour the steeped hibiscus tea into a serving pitcher. Add the lime juice and halves. Add ice and stir until chilled. Add the sparkling wine and serve immediately.

Passion Fruit and Chiltepín Spritz Serves 4

Chiltepín peppers grow wild in the Southwest, and this drink is wild. Tantalizing on the taste buds, it starts off sweet and then the heat kicks in. Tart passion fruit makes for a beautiful presentation when served up family style in a large pitcher, but if you can't find passion fruit puree, lemon or lime juice with a splash of your favorite tropical fruit juice makes a good substitute. Just be careful; chiltepines can take you for a ride.

1 cup vodka or sparkling water

1 cup passion fruit puree

1¼ cups *chiltepín* syrup (recipe follows)

1 lime, juiced

¼ cup Grand Marnier
or fresh squeezed orange juice

Fill 4 pint-size mason jars with ice and divide the vodka or sparkling water, passion fruit puree, *chiltepín* syrup, and fresh squeezed lime juice. Stir well and top with Grand Marnier or orange juice.

Garnish with saguaro seeds.

Chiltepín Syrup Makes 3½ cups

Chiltepín syrup is a great way to add some heat to a cocktail. It has a real kick, so go easy on it.

2 cups water

2¼ cups sugar

2 or 3 *chiltepín* pods

Heat the water and sugar over medium heat in a saucepot. Once the sugar is dissolved, add the *chiltepines*, remove from heat, and cool.

Puree in the blender until smooth. Strain, cool, and store in a tightly covered glass jar in the refrigerator for up to three days.

Chiles

We use them in everything from drinks to desserts, so let's jump into this spicy topic here at the very beginning. There are thousands of different varieties of chiles in the world, and they all have their own particular flavor profiles and heat indexes. In the Southwest, we use a wide range, but there are a few that are popular and easy to find.

Anaheim It's long and bright green with a mild, fruity flavor. You can roast and peel them and use them like their spicier cousins, and they also make a nice non-spicy relleno.

Poblano/Ancho Fresh, it's a poblano, a large, dark green chile perfect for stuffing. Dry it and it changes its name to ancho. It's at home in everything and makes a nice chile powder. The heat is just enough to get your attention, but not enough to hurt you.

Cascabel Small, round, and deep red, these chiles add a comforting warmth and rich flavor. They're usually used in dried form.

Chilaca/Pasilla (or Chile Negro) Fresh chilacas ripen from a dark green to black, and when dried, become pasillas. They're only moderately hot, and dried pasillas are one component of mole.

Chiltepín This little hottie is a native of the desert Southwest and Mexico and grows wild in Northern Sonora and parts of the Southwest United States. It's a tiny red ball of fire, and you can usually find them dried or pickled. If you live in a warm climate, you can grow your own. The shrub is pretty, especially when it's covered in little bright red berries. These are really hot, so when you use them in a dish, go easy.

Jalapeño/Chipotle Jalapeños are probably the most widely used chile in American cooking. You can use them fresh or pickled and they add a nice heat to pizza, burgers, or even pasta sauces. When it's smoked and dried, the sleek jalapeño turns into a chipotle, a shriveled-up, little brown thing that adds a smoky kick to sauces and stews.

Mirasol/Guajillo Mirasol means "see the sun," and these bright red chiles grow upside down on the plant. They have a nice fruity flavor and medium heat. Dry them and they become guajillos, which you'll find used plenty in this book. I like the flavor and the nice amount of spice.

Habanero Like the chiltepín, they've written songs about this one (Hot, Hot, Hot!). These are a really pretty pepper, usually bright orange or yellow, but you want to go easy, because you don't want to have regrets later.

Mulato This is a close relative of the poblano/ancho, and you'll usually find it dried. Unlike the ancho, which is dark red, the mulato is almost black. The flavor is a little more assertive, but the heat is about the same. This one is frequently used in moles.

Jalapeño and Valencia Jam Spritzer Serves 2

This is a fun one for the pool. It is simple to make as well as refreshing. You'll get a little wake up from the jalapeños, but the heat is a nice complement to the sweetness of the oranges. Although you can probably find Valencia oranges all year long, they're best March through June when they're in season. They're full of juice and have a sweetness unlike any other orange.

½ cup Valencia orange juice

Zest from one Valencia orange

1 tablespoon minced jalapeño

¼ cup sugar

¼ teaspoon agar-agar (see note)

1 cup lemon-lime soda

1 cup sauvignon blanc

Orange twist and jalapeño slices, for garnish

Heat the orange juice and zest, jalapeño, and sugar over medium heat in a sauté pan until the sugar is dissolved. Add the agar-agar and cook an additional 30 seconds until dissolved. Remove from the heat and chill until jelled.

Place equal amounts of the soda and sauvignon blanc into two tall Collins glasses filled with ice. Add 2 tablespoons of the reserved jam to each and stir well. Garnish with orange and jalapeño.

Note: Agar-agar is a natural vegetarian gelatin extracted from red algae. It helps jellies set quickly and stay set at room temperature. Use the powdered form available at Asian groceries, health food stores, or online. (See Sources, page 144)

Black Rice Horchata with Cinnamon Makes 2 quarts

Some call this my signature drink. The waiting period is far too long for this cocktail, so that's why I usually make a double batch...or triple. The combination of forbidden black rice, almonds, and cinnamon creates a silky texture that works well with cinnamon-infused whiskey. No one is going to judge you if you replace your morning coffee with one of these.

9 cups water, divided

1 cup black rice, uncooked

1 cup basmati rice, uncooked

1 cup almonds

1 cinnamon stick

1½ cups sugar

¼ teaspoon vanilla extract

Cinnamon-infused whiskey (optional, see note)

Cinnamon stick, for garnish

Mix 4 cups of water, uncooked black and basmati rice, almonds, cinnamon stick, sugar, and vanilla in a large pitcher and refrigerate overnight.

The next day, add 5 cups of water and puree in the blender until very smooth. Strain the mixture through a cheesecloth or fine strainer and chill.

Pour over ice and add a shot of cinnamon-infused whiskey, if desired. Serve with a cinnamon stick garnish.

Note: To make cinnamon-infused whiskey, add a few cinnamon sticks to a bottle of whiskey and allow to sit in a dark cool place for 2 to 3 days. Strain to remove the cinnamon and replace the whiskey in the bottle.

Sweet and Sour and Bitter Margarita Makes 3 quarts

Get rid of that bottled margarita mix hiding in the fridge. Fresh is the only way to go. And besides, we're not going to waste any of the fruit because we're going to add some bitter to that sweet and sour mix. You'll need a high-powered blender to puree the skins, pith, and seeds of the citrus. Get creative and mix it up by using tangerines or grapefruit. You can't go wrong.

1⅓ cups sugar

1 cup water

Pinch of salt

1 lime

½ orange

¾ cup lemon juice

¼ cup orange juice

1¼ cups lime juice

2 or 3 dashes of bitters

2 cups silver tequila

1 cup triple sec

Heat the sugar, water, and salt over medium heat in a saucepot. Once the sugar and salt are dissolved, remove from the heat and cool slightly.

Dice the lime and orange, peel and all, and add to the blender along with the warm syrup and juice. Puree until smooth.

When the citrus syrup has cooled completely, mix the bitters, tequila, and triple sec in a large pitcher. Stir and add ice. Serve in margarita glasses with a wedge of citrus. You can salt the rims if you like, but keep in mind that there's already salt in the syrup.

Pomegranate Sour Serves 2

This cocktail took the gold. Seriously, it was named the World's Greatest Margarita 2012 at the Seventh Annual World Margarita Championship right here in Tucson. Tucson is the world margarita capital, and there are plenty to choose from. In this one, we mix in some pomegranate juice and a little white balsamic vinegar to give you that lip-puckering, margarita good time. Look for a *reposado* (rested) tequila that's been aged at least two months. Aging mellows out the sharpness and bite of the tequila, and (with a mid-range tequila) the price is right. The balsamic vinegar brings this whole drink together. We source a local product, but any white balsamic vinegar will do.

1 cup citrus syrup (page 12)

½ cup Penasco or other *reposado* tequila

¼ cup Grand Marnier

2 dashes of Queen Creek pomegranate or other white balsamic vinegar

1 splash of Pom or other pomegranate juice

2 tablespoons fresh pomegranate seeds

Pour the citrus syrup, tequila, Grand Marnier, vinegar, and pomegranate juice into an ice-filled shaker. Shake hard and strain into two unsalted martini glasses.

Garnish with fresh pomegranate seeds.

Tequila is a clear liquor distilled from the blue agave plant, and most people think it's the official liquor of the Southwest, even though almost all of it is distilled in Mexico. Mexican law says that anything labeled as tequila must contain at least 51 percent agave, with sugar cane and other additives permitted (then called a *mixto*). Some premium brands are 100 percent agave, and they definitely taste better. If a label says 100% blue agave, you know it's the pure stuff. If it just says tequila, it's a *mixto*. In addition, you'll find tequila with five different labels:

Blanco or plata (white or silver) These can be either 100 percent or *mixto*, and they're aged in stainless steel for no more than 60 days. They're perfectly clear, have a vegetal agave flavor, and are great for mixing.

Gold This is a *mixto*, and hasn't been aged at all. The color and some of the flavor comes from caramel or other colorings. These are usually inexpensive and what you find in margaritas at college bars.

Reposado (rested) Now you're talking. This can be a *mixto* or 100 percent, and it's been aged in wood casks for at least two months, sometimes up to nine. A nice *reposado* is good for sipping.

Anejo (old) These tequilas are aged in oak or old bourbon barrels for anywhere from a year to three, and they're dark and smoky. Sip this one out of a snifter so you can get the full experience.

Extra Anejo These are aged for more than three years in oak or old bourbon barrels, and they more closely resemble whiskey than tequila. Most of the agave flavor is gone, replaced by the complexities of the cask, but they're usually smooth and rich.

And then there's mezcal. All tequilas are mezcal, but not all mezcals are tequila. While tequila is made in certain regions and only from the blue agave, mezcal can be made from other varieties of the maguey (agave) and in other regions. It has a strong smoky flavor and is usually consumed in shots, not mixed or sipped.

Prickly Pear Mojito Serves 2

Everyone loves mojitos, and this one adds a touch of the desert to the rum and mint. No skimping here—you have to use fresh prickly pear cactus fruit puree for the foam. If you don't have prickly pear cactus growing in your backyard, then go for the frozen stuff online. Steer away from prickly pear syrup—it's mostly sugar.

1¼ cups water, divided

1 teaspoon powdered gelatin

¾ cup sugar

¼ cup fresh prickly pear juice

2 lime wedges

½ cup light rum

¼ cup lime juice

2 tablespoons mint syrup (recipe follows)

splash, club soda

Place ¾ cup of water and gelatin in a mixing bowl and whisk until dissolved. Heat the remaining water with the sugar and prickly pear juice until dissolved. Pour over the gelatin mixture and whisk until fully melted. You may need to apply low heat to get it to melt completely. Once the mixture is completely melted, pour it into a cream whipper and charge twice. Let cool slightly for the foam to thicken.

Divide the limes into two mixing glasses and muddle well. Add the divided rum, lime juice, and mint syrup. Add ice and shake well. Pour into two rocks glasses, add a splash of club soda, and apply the prickly pear foam over the top for garnish.

✓Mint Syrup Makes ¾ cup

This syrup will hold in the refrigerator for weeks and is a great way to get the maximum flavor from your mint.

½ cup water

½ cup sugar

20 fresh mint leaves

In a small pan over medium heat, bring the water and sugar to a boil. When the sugar is dissolved, remove from heat, add the mint leaves, and cool. Puree and then store in a tightly sealed glass jar.

Chef's Habanero Manhattan Serves 2

The guests have left, the kitchen is cleaned, and the prep lists have been written for the next morning. The last things on a chef's to-do list are to place a few last-minute seafood and produce orders and have a cocktail. I have to be back in the office in the morning, so I tend to have just one drink, and it has to be good and strong. We make this in a classic way, but add a punch of subtle heat to the bitters with a little habanero. This drink is really all about the rye whiskey and making Chef happy.

4 ounces rye whiskey

2 ounces Italian sweet vermouth

4 dashes habanero angostura bitters (see note)

2–4 naturally preserved cherries

Pour the rye, vermouth, and bitters into a mixing glass along with several large chunks of ice. Stir for 20 to 30 seconds until very cold. Strain into 2 chilled martini glasses and garnish with 2 naturally preserved cherries.

Note: To spice up the bitters, add half a fresh habanero to a bottle of angostura bitters. Cap it and let it sit in a cool, dark place for about a week. Remove the habanero when it reaches the level of heat you like.

THE IN-BETWEENS

Let's be honest. I skip meals every day. I don't think it would even be possible for me, or any chef for that matter, to sit down and eat three proper meals a day with a few snacks in between. When I get home from a busy shift, dinner time has long passed, and I'm into late-night snack mode with a proper beverage to match. The in-betweens are all about the scratch snacks that help us get through our day or beat those cravings. The older I get, the more I realize how important it is to replace the processed snack foods with real food. This doesn't mean it has to be celery and carrots or bacon jam and cheese; it just has to be real food.

Southwestern Spiced Nuts Makes 6 cups

The Southwest has an abundance of nut trees and farms. Acres of pecan and pistachio grow just a few miles from my house, and we use the nuts with abandon. This spice blend is sweet, smoky, and spicy. Wrap these up in small gift bags for a treat for the neighbors or eat 'em all!

2 egg whites

½ cup sugar

2 teaspoons pepper

1½ tablespoons salt

2 teaspoons cayenne

2 teaspoons ground coriander

2 tablespoons chile powder

1 cup almonds

1 cup cashews

2 cups walnuts

½ cup peanuts

1 cup pecans

Preheat oven to 350 degrees F.

In a large bowl, whisk the egg whites until light and fluffy. Add the sugar, pepper, salt, cayenne, coriander, and chile powder and beat until smooth. Fold in the nuts and gently mix until coated.

Line a baking sheet with parchment or a silicon baking mat. Spread the nut mixture evenly on the baking sheet. Bake for 6 to 8 minutes or until golden, stirring once or twice during baking.

Let cool before eating. Store in an airtight container.

Toast 'n' Jam Makes 2 loaves (9" x 5") and 2 cups of jam

Nothing beats having freshly baked bread at home except for freshly baked bread and jam. This is a staple in my house. White Sonora wheat is a dryland variety that fed most of the Western United States and Mexico until it fell out of favor and was replaced by commercial varieties. With the help of Native Seeds/SEARCH and the US Ark of Taste from Slow Food USA, white Sonora is making a comeback and is increasingly sought after because of its drought tolerance and exquisite taste and texture. This loaf will balance nicely with the sweet, tart, and spicy jam. Just don't get too excited and stick the fork in the toaster.

Bread

¾ cup warm water
(105 to 115 degrees F)

1 tablespoon dry yeast

1 tablespoon sugar

1½ cups buttermilk,
at room temperature

2 tablespoons melted butter

3 tablespoons honey

1 tablespoon salt

6 to 6¼ cups white Sonora
wheat flour or bread flour

1 egg

Bread: In a small bowl, whisk together the warm water, yeast, and sugar. Allow to sit for 8 to 10 minutes until it becomes foamy.

In a the bowl of a stand mixer with a dough hook attachment, place the yeast mixture, buttermilk, butter, honey, salt, and 1 cup of the flour. Mix on low speed until combined. Slowly add the remaining flour 1 cup at a time until the dough forms a ball. You may not need the last ½ cup of flour. Knead the dough in the mixer for 4 minutes or until the dough springs back when poked with your finger. Remove from the mixer bowl and shape into a smooth ball. Place in a lightly oiled bowl and cover with a kitchen towel.

Allow the covered dough to rise in a warm place for 1 to 1½ hours until doubled in size.

Divide the dough into two pieces and gently shape it to fit into two 9 by 5-inch loaf pans. Cover the pans with a kitchen towel and allow them to rise once more, 30–45 minutes, or until the dough reaches to the top of the pans.

Preheat the oven to 350 degrees F.

Whisk the egg until smooth and brush lightly over each loaf to glaze.

Place the pans in the oven and bake 45 minutes or until the loaf begins to pull away from the sides of the bread pan. Remove from the oven, remove the loaves from the pans, and allow to cool on a rack before slicing.

(continued)

The Slow Food Ark of Taste

The Ark of Taste is a catalog of more than 1,100 food products and traditions from more than 50 countries that are in danger of being lost. The Ark is part of the Slow Food movement, based in Italy and dedicated to preserving biodiversity and gastronomic traditions. I use many of the regional and local Ark products, such as Sonoran white wheat, tepary beans, and chiltepínes, because the more we use them, the more reason there will be for farmers to grow them. They also taste great, and if you're going to cook with local products, it's nice to know indigenous cooks have been using them for years. It adds another level of authenticity to the food. You can learn more about the Ark of Taste and about Slow Food in general on the Slow Food USA website. www.slowfoodusa.org

The Jam

2 ounces *guajillo* chiles

2 cups hot water

1 cup sugar

1 pint blueberries

1 pint blackberries

1 pinch of salt

⅛ teaspoon agar-agar (page 17)

The Jam: While the bread is rising and baking, make the jam.

Place the *guajillo* chiles, sugar, and water in a saucepot and bring to a simmer for 5 minutes. Remove from the heat, remove the stems from the chiles, and puree the mixture in a blender until smooth.

Mix the blueberries, blackberries, salt, and agar-agar together in a saucepot and add the *guajillo* puree. Bring to a simmer and cook until reduced by half. Mix well. Remove from heat and cool. Store in a glass jar in the refrigerator for up to 2 weeks.

Slice the bread, toast it under the broiler, and then spread with the jam.

Bacon + Truffle + Mole Popcorn Makes 6 cups

Oh, yeah! These are a few of my favorite things. Salty bacon, earthy truffles, and sweet 'n' spicy mole will turn your popcorn-eating world upside down. The fun here is turning bacon fat and truffle oil into powder. Yes, powder. Tapioca maltrodextrin, a natural food starch, actually absorbs the fat and encapsulates it into a powder form. Once water molecules from the moisture in your mouth touch the powder, it transforms back into its natural state and flavors the heck out of that popcorn. You'll be sneaking this one into the movies!

2 tablespoons bacon fat

2 tablespoons truffle oil

1½ cups tapioca maltrodextrin, or as needed (see note)

1 tablespoon ancho chile powder

1 tablespoon red chile powder

¼ teaspoon cayenne or jalapeño powder

1 tablespoon Dutch cocoa powder

2 tablespoons *pepitas* (page 48), toasted and crushed into a powder

3 tablespoons vegetable oil

¾ cup popcorn kernels

2 tablespoons butter, melted

Salt to taste

Make the bacon and truffle powders by placing the bacon fat and the truffle oil into two separate small bowls. Slowly whisk in the tapioca maltrodextrin, adding in small amounts just until the fats transform into powders, about ¾ cup per bowl.

Make mole powder by blending the ancho chile powder, red chile powder, cayenne, cocoa, and *pepitas* in a spice grinder until smooth.

Heat a wide skillet to medium high heat. Add the vegetable oil. Once the oil shimmers, add the corn kernels and cover. Shake the pan every few seconds and wait for a popping sound. Continue shaking until the popping subsides to 1 kernel every 4 to 5 seconds. Remove from the heat and season with melted butter and salt to taste. Divide the popped corn into three equal batches and season separately with the bacon powder, truffle powder, and mole powder to desired taste.

Note: Tapioca maltodextrin is available online and can be used to turn any fat-based food into powder. Try peanut butter, Nutella, yogurt, olive oil—get crazy and experiment!

Escabeche Pickles Makes 2 quarts

In my home refrigerator you'll always find salumi. It lasts forever and makes a great little snack, especially when paired with some spicy mustard and pickled vegetables to cut through the salty richness of the cured meat. Use whatever vegetables you like and don't be afraid to play around with the mix. These can be eaten immediately or within several days. They'll only get better as they have a chance to hang out in the brine.

½ cup pickling spice

1 quart cider vinegar

1 quart water

2 jalapeños, sliced

3 sprigs thyme

1 tablespoon salt

½ cup sugar

½ cauliflower, florets only

1 dozen baby carrots, halved lengthwise

2 ribs celery, peeled and cut into 1-inch pieces

12 garlic cloves

12 cornichon pickles

6 small sweet peppers, whole

12 olives

1 cup small mushrooms, such as enoki or oyster

6 radishes, halved

In a large saucepan, heat the pickling spice, cider vinegar, water, jalapeño, thyme, salt, and sugar until dissolved. Set aside until slightly cool and then strain.

Pack the raw vegetables into two 1-quart Mason jars and cover with the warm pickling liquid. Let cool to room temperature. Place the lids on the jars and refrigerate. For best flavor, allow to sit for 2 to 3 days in the refrigerator before serving.

✓ Roasted Pepper Hummus Serves 4–6

Adding grilled vegetables to hummus creates complexity and dimension in this simple, peasant food. For this one, we've chosen sweet red bell peppers. Leave some of the charred skin on to add that grilled flavor. You can substitute any sweet peppers, but I enjoy the balance that red bells give this snack.

2 red bell peppers

1 can chickpeas (15-ounce), drained, with 2 tablespoons of the liquid reserved

1 garlic clove, sliced

¼ cup tahini

½ teaspoon ground cumin

1 tablespoon lemon juice

¼ cup blended oil (page 51)

¼ teaspoon salt

Pinch of pepper

Pita chips or crudités, for serving

Char the bell peppers over an open flame until they are entirely blackened. Place the peppers in a mixing bowl, cover with plastic wrap, and let cool.

Remove the skin, seeds, and stems from the peppers.

In a food processor, puree the peppers, chickpeas and liquid, garlic, tahini, cumin, lemon juice, and oil for 1 minute. Scrape down the bowl with a rubber spatula. Puree until smooth. Season with salt and pepper. Serve with pita chips or fresh vegetables for dipping.

Salsa Fresca Makes 4 cups ✓

Salsa fresca gives a burst of freshness to any dish. It's great on eggs in the morning or enchiladas at night. If you like it extra spicy leave the seeds in the jalapeño.

1 pound vine-ripened tomatoes, seeded and finely diced

½ cup minced red onion

½ cup diced yellow bell pepper

1 clove garlic, minced

2 tablespoons chopped cilantro

¼ cup fresh squeezed lime juice

1 jalapeño, seeded and minced

1 tablespoon olive oil

2 teaspoons salt

½ teaspoon pepper

In a medium bowl, combine all ingredients. Stir well and adjust the seasonings, if necessary. Chill for at least 1 hour.

One of the ultimate on-the-go snacks is chips and salsa. You could hit the convenience store on the way home and grab some cardboard chips and a jar of bland salsa, or you could take a few minutes and make your own. It's easy to fry up some tortilla wedges in a little hot oil in a skillet, and then chop up some tomatoes, onion, garlic, and peppers. You can do a fresh uncooked salsa (*fresca*) or cook it for a different flavor entirely. And if you keep a supply on hand in the refrigerator, you'll always have it when the yearning for tacos strikes. And where there are tacos, you might find tequila!

Salsa Verde Makes 2 quarts

This is one of the classic sauces used in the Southwest. You can put it on everything from the pork butt on page 119 to scrambled eggs, tacos, burritos, and even grilled fish.

2½ pounds tomatillos, husked

½ pound poblanos

½ jalapeño

1 medium onion

¼ cup blended oil

2 teaspoons salt

½ teaspoon pepper

2 scallions, diced

½ bunch cilantro, chopped

2 tablespoons lime juice

Preheat oven to 400 degrees F.

Chop the tomatillos, poblanos, jalapeño, and onion into uniform chunks. Toss with the oil, salt, and pepper and roast 22 to 25 minutes or until blackened. Remove from the oven and transfer to a large bowl. Puree with a stick blender so the salsa remains a bit chunky. Add the diced scallions, cilantro, and lime juice. Taste and adjust the salt and pepper, then chill.

Taco Sauce Makes 4 cups

There's nothing better than homemade taco sauce. Keep this one in the fridge for when the mood strikes.

¼ cup vegetable oil

2 tablespoons minced shallot

2 teaspoons minced garlic

1 tablespoon dried oregano

1 teaspoon ground cumin

2 tablespoons chile powder

1½ cups tomato puree

2 cups chicken stock (page 95)
or dark vegetable stock (page 44)

1 teaspoon salt

⅛ teaspoon pepper

1 tablespoon cornstarch

1 tablespoon cold water

In a medium pan, heat the oil and add the shallot and garlic. Sauté until tender. Stir in the oregano, cumin, and chile powder, and then add the tomato puree and stock. Simmer for 15 minutes. Add salt and pepper and remove from heat. Cool slightly. Puree in a blender and then strain. Return to the pan and simmer for a few minutes, then puree and strain again. If the sauce needs thickening, make a slurry by stirring the cornstarch and cold water into a paste, bring the sauce to a simmer, and whisk in the slurry. Cook until the sauce is thickened.

Rattlesnake Bean Dip + Salsa Amarillo Makes 4 cups of each

A duet of dips here, and no rattlesnakes were harmed in the making. Rattlesnake beans are indigenous to the Southwest and get their name from the pattern on the bean. These small beans, a hybrid of the pinto, have a tangy flavor and work well pureed. Match this up with a bright yellow salsa with a kick and subtle sweetness, and serve them both with homemade tortilla chips.

Rattlesnake Bean Dip

¾ cup dried rattlesnake beans

1 onion, diced

3 garlic cloves, minced

1 jalapeño, sliced

1 fresh poblano, diced

2 tablespoons olive oil

½ bunch cilantro, chopped

1 lime, juice and zest

1 tablespoon ground cumin

2 tablespoons salt

1 teaspoon pepper

Bean Dip: Wash and pick through the beans to eliminate any rocks or other debris. Place in a large bowl and cover with water. Soak 8 hours.

Drain and rinse the beans. Place in a large saucepan and cover with water. Heat on medium high until simmering. Maintain a simmer for 30 to 45 minutes, adding water if needed. Cook until tender. Remove from heat and allow to cool.

Sauté the onion, garlic, jalapeño, and poblano in olive oil over low heat until tender, about 10 to 15 minutes.

Strain the beans and reserve the liquid. Place the beans, sautéed vegetables, cilantro, lime juice and zest, cumin, salt, and pepper into a blender and puree. Add about ¼ cup of the reserved bean broth to achieve your desired consistency.

Salsa Amarillo

8 yellow bell peppers

1 onion, diced

2 garlic cloves, chopped

2 tablespoons blended oil

1 teaspoon cayenne

1 teaspoon ground cumin

1 teaspoon ground coriander

2 limes, juice and zest

1½ cups water

2 tablespoons rice wine vinegar

1 tablespoon salt

1 teaspoon pepper

Salsa Amarillo: Char the bell peppers over an open flame until blackened on the outside. Place the peppers in a paper bag and let them steam for 15 minutes. Remove them from the bag and remove the charred skins, seeds, and stems.

Sauté the onion and garlic in the blended oil until tender. Stir in the cayenne, cumin, and coriander and cook another minute. Add the lime juice and zest, water, vinegar, salt, and pepper. Bring to a simmer and cook for 5 minutes. Remove from heat and allow to cool at room temperature.

Puree all ingredients before serving at room temperature.

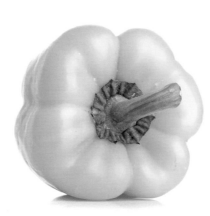

Smoked Salmon Prickly Pear Spread Serves 6–8

Bringing a beautiful spread to a party shows a little more thought than just grabbing a premade crudité platter on the way over. With its stunning colors and robust flavors, this one will be a hit at your next event. Curing and smoking the salmon takes several days, so if you don't have time to do it yourself, it's fine to buy prepared smoked salmon.

1½ tablespoons Basic Cure (recipe follows)

1 tablespoon brown sugar

1 salmon fillet (6 ounce), or 4 ounces smoked salmon, thinly sliced

1 pound cream cheese

½ cup fresh prickly pear juice

2 red bell peppers, sliced

1 zucchini, sliced lengthwise

1 teaspoon salt

¼ teaspoon pepper

¼ cup blended oil

Crackers or warmed flatbread for serving

Mix the Basic Cure with the brown sugar. Sprinkle over the salmon fillet and coat well.

Place the salmon in a nonreactive container and refrigerate for 36 hours or until the thickest part of the salmon feels dense. Rinse well under cold water and pat dry.

Let the salmon air dry in the refrigerator for at least 4 hours.

Remove the salmon from the refrigerator and slice thinly. Place the slices in a 1-gallon zippered plastic bag. Use The Smoking Gun to pump the desired smoke into the bag and then seal it. Let the smoke permeate the salmon for 8–10 minutes. Remove the smoked salmon from the plastic bag and chill for 15 minutes.

Combine the cream cheese with the prickly pear juice until well blended.

Line a 4-by-8-inch terrine mold with plastic wrap. Place one even layer of bell peppers on the bottom, followed by a layer of zucchini and a layer of salmon Use a pastry bag to pipe on an even layer of cream cheese about ¼-inch thick. Alternate the layers using the vegetables, smoked salmon, and cream cheese.

Once the terrine is full, fold the plastic over and place the weight on top. Refrigerate for at least 24 hours.

To serve, remove the terrine from the mold and discard the plastic wrap. Slice into 2-inch pieces with a sharp knife. Serve with crackers or warmed flatbread.

Basic Cure Makes about 1 cup

This is perfect for curing salmon, trout, or pork. Pink curing salt is a combination of table salt and sodium nitrite—it's not the same as pink finishing salt, which is an unrefined salt made pink by the mineral content. The two are not interchangeable. If you want to skip the nitrites for a more natural cure, leave it out.

½ **pound kosher salt**

½ **cup sugar**

1 ounce pink curing salt

Mix all ingredients well and store in an airtight container.

To use, dredge the meat in 2 ounces of cure mixture for every 5 pounds of meat. Allow meat to cure in a nonreactive pan until firm. The time depends on the thickness of the meat.

The Best Guacamole Serves 4–6

Okay, maybe I'm a little biased here, but seriously, this is good. There are no fillers in this guacamole—just creamy avocados and complementing flavors. Sprinkle the tortilla chips with a little smoked sea salt and you're going to be very happy.

5 avocados

1 tablespoon lime juice

½ teaspoon ground cumin

2 teaspoons minced jalapeño

1 teaspoon salt

½ teaspoon fresh ground pepper

2 tablespoons cotija cheese

1 teaspoon blended oil

2 tablespoons finely chopped cilantro

Remove the pit and skin of the avocados and chop them into a mixing bowl. Add the lime juice, cumin, jalapeño, salt, pepper, cheese, oil, and cilantro. Using a fork, mash the ingredients together until smooth and mixed well.

Serve with tortilla chips.

FROM THE GARDEN

A great dish starts with the soil. Imagine how you treat yourself in a comfy bed with oversized sheets and a plush pillow. Vegetables, fruits, and greens deserve the same lush foundation to live in, and that's why organic is the way to go. Organic production on small farms is all about building and preserving the soil to get the most nutritious and delicious produce. I source all of my produce from small local vendors because I can see and taste the difference. I develop relationships with farmers and see the passion they have for what they're doing. Each farmer can tell me exactly what's at its peak and whether or not they'll have a supply in the following weeks. Sometimes buying from the small local producers can bring its own set of challenges. One farm that I use for breakfast radishes was robbed by a gang of groundhogs, so I took the radishes off the menu, replaced them with pickled chard stems, and sent the farmers a stuffed groundhog.

Sweet Potato Angel Hair with Chipotle Cream Sauce Serves 4–6

Surprise your dinner party guests with this play on pasta. Using a Benriner turning slicer, make thin spiral cuts of any root vegetable to resemble thin angel hair pasta. Cook the "pasta" in a chipotle cream sauce to add a smoky flavor, and for an extra wow factor, use a carving fork to spin the pasta into a little nest and crack in an egg yolk. As with any pasta, I suggest you pile on some fresh-grated hard cheese. A nice, aged dry jack will do the trick.

½ large onion, diced

2 ounces blended oil

½ cup dry white wine

1 cup heavy cream

1¼ cups chicken (page 95)
or dark vegetable stock (page 44)

3 chipotles in adobo

1 pound sweet potatoes, peeled

1 teaspoon salt

¼ teaspoon pepper

½ cup dry jack cheese,
peeled and grated

Over medium heat in a large pan, sauté the onion in the oil until tender. Add the white wine and cook until reduced by three quarters, about 8 minutes. Remove from heat and add the cream, stock, and chipotles. Transfer to a blender and puree. Transfer back to the pot and bring to a simmer.

Slice the ends of the sweet potato so they're flat. Use a Japanese Benriner slicer to spiral cut the sweet potato, using the medium serrated blade. Add the sweet potato to the cream sauce and season with salt and pepper. Allow the sauce to cook and tenderize the sweet potato for 15–20 minutes. Once the sauce is mostly soaked up and the sweet potato is tender, taste and season again if needed.

Transfer to a serving dish and top with cheese.

Dark Vegetable Stock Makes 2½ quarts

When you're cooking for your vegetarian friends, this makes a good substitute for meat stock. It also adds great taste and color to those vegetarian dishes that beg for moisture. Vegetable stock can lose its flavor quickly, so I suggest using it immediately or putting it straight into the freezer.

¼ cup vegetable oil

2 pounds leeks, sliced

1¼ pounds carrots, large dice

1¼ pounds onions, large dice

1 bulb fennel, sliced

½ pound button mushrooms, cleaned and sliced

2 ears of corn, cut in half

1 bunch parsley, chopped

Making Stock

A good stock is the starting point for sauces, soups, gravies, and braises, and it's a simple kitchen trick to make your own. Once you do, you'll never buy it at the store again. The two most versatile stocks are chicken and vegetable, but it's always nice to have a quart or two of seafood and veal stock on hand, too. Keep them in your freezer and a hearty soup is just a handful of chopped vegetables away.

Preheat oven to 350 degrees F.

Heat the vegetable oil in a roasting pan and add the leeks, carrots, onions, fennel, mushrooms, and corn. Roast until the vegetables are caramelized and tender, about 20 minutes.

Remove from the oven and place the roasted vegetables into an 8-quart stockpot. Cover with 3 quarts of cold water. Bring to a simmer and cook for 45 minutes, skimming the top periodically.

Remove from the heat, add the chopped parsley, and allow to sit for 15 minutes while the particles in the stock settle at the bottom. Using a ladle, remove the stock from the top, leaving the sediment on the bottom to be discarded. Strain and cool.

Freeze for up to 2 months or refrigerate for use within 1 day.

Winter Kale with Pecans, Dates, and Beets Serves 4–6

This simple recipe lets the food speak for itself. The careful preparation of each individual ingredient allows for a harmonious whole when they're put together. Focus on a diversity of colors, textures, and flavors. I like to use a variety of baby beets in this recipe. Don't be afraid to chop the beet greens and toss 'em into the mix.

1 bunch rainbow kale

1 pound baby beets

1 egg white

1 tablespoon chile powder

1 teaspoon salt

1 tablespoon sugar

1 cup pecans

2 tablespoons olive oil

½ cup dates, seeded and chopped

1 teaspoon salt

¼ teaspoon pepper

1 lemon, zest and juice

Preheat the oven to 350 degrees F.

Remove the kale leaves from the stems and chop the leaves into large pieces. Thinly slice the stems and add to the leaves. Remove the beet tops and chop. Add them to kale and set aside.

Wrap the beets in foil and roast until tender, 20 to 30 minutes.

Meanwhile, whip the egg white to soft peaks. Fold in the chile powder, salt, and sugar. Fold in the pecans and spread them onto a parchment-lined baking sheet. Place in the oven and bake until dry, about 8 to 10 minutes. Remove from the oven and set aside.

Remove the beets from the oven and let cool. Unwrap and peel away the skin. Cut into 1-inch chunks.

Heat a large skillet over medium heat and add the olive oil. When the oil shimmers, add the kale and beet greens and wilt until just warmed through.

In a large bowl, mix the greens, beets, dates, and pecans. Season with salt and pepper and sprinkle with lemon zest and juice. Serve immediately.

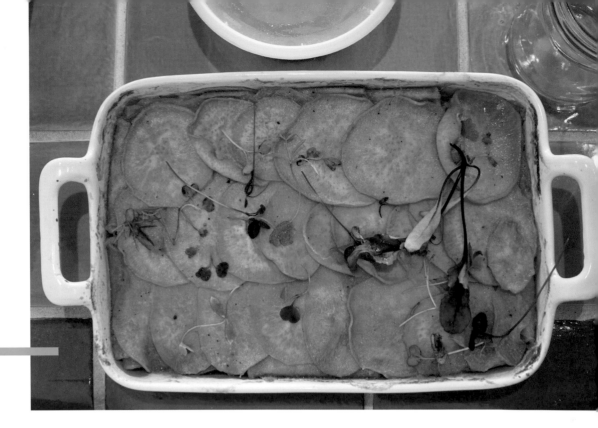

Yam and Ginger-Jalapeño Pavé Serves 8–10

Sit the old-school potato gratin on the bench and send this all-star into the game. *Pavé* describes a square or rectangle cut. When you press the layers of this dish, you get shingled layers of sweet and subtle spice. Pair with roasted pork loin, and you've got yourself a winning team.

2 ounces blended oil (see note)

3 tablespoons minced fresh ginger

⅓ cup minced jalapeño, seeds and ribs removed

¼ cup minced onion

2 garlic cloves, minced

2 pounds yams, peeled

2 cups cream

¾ cup chicken (page 95) or dark vegetable stock (page 44)

1 tablespoon salt

1 teaspoon pepper

1 ounce butter

1 ounce blended oil

(continued)

Preheat the oven to 350 degrees F.

Heat the oil in a medium sauté pan over medium heat, then sauté the ginger, jalapeño, onion, and garlic until tender, about 5 minutes. Remove from heat.

Peel and slice the yams in half crosswise. Use a Japanese mandolin to slice 1/8-inch-thick slices of the yams. Mix the yams and ginger mixture together.

In a large measuring cup, mix the cream and stock together. Season well with salt and pepper. Taste. The mixture should taste heavily seasoned.

In a large mixing bowl, stir together the sweet potato mixture and the cream sauce.

Oil a 2-quart rectangular baking dish and place the yams in layers, pressing down, as the cream mixture can make the yams swim towards the top. Continue layering the yams until the pan is full. Give the top a final press to ensure the yams are tightly fit in the baking dish. Pour any remaining liquid over the top. Cover with foil. Place in the oven and bake 35 minutes.

Remove the foil and turn the oven up to 375 degrees F. Bake an additional 15 to 20 minutes or until tender. Remove from the oven and let cool 10 minutes.

Place plastic wrap over the top of the dish and place a heavy baking dish of the same size on top of the plastic. Let stand 15 minutes on the counter to cool. The weight of the dish will press the yams and create a dense pavé.

Remove the extra dish and the plastic and cut and serve immediately.

To serve later, cool in the refrigerator with the weight on top. After the pavé is completely chilled, remove the weight and the plastic and invert the pavé onto a cutting board. Remove the dish and cut into small squares, 3 by 3 inches.

Preheat the oven to 350 degrees F.

In an oven-proof sauté pan, melt the butter and oil. When hot, add the squares cut-side-down and brown. Turn them over, and place the pan in the oven. Cook until warm throughout, about 8 minutes.

Note: Blended oil (page 51) is a combination of canola and olive oil, usually in a 75:25 ratio. It's excellent for baking and sautéing.

Spaghetti Squash and Cilantro Pesto Serves 6

Time to dress up that boring spaghetti squash. Be careful to not overcook it—you don't want it mushy. By both roasting and sautéing, you'll achieve that steam-roasted flavor with accents of brown butter and herbaceous cilantro. This is great by itself, but don't be afraid to top it off with ancho-braised lamb shanks (pages 116–117). Yum!

1 spaghetti squash (5–6 pounds)

¼ cup olive oil

1 tablespoon salt

1 teaspoon pepper

2 tablespoons butter

½ cup cilantro pesto (recipe follows)

¼ cup toasted *pepitas*, for garnish (see note)

Preheat oven to 350 degrees F.

Cut the spaghetti squash in half lengthwise. Drizzle the cut side with olive oil and sprinkle with salt and pepper. Place flesh-side down on a parchment-lined baking sheet.

Bake for 15 to 20 minutes until tender. Remove from the oven and cool at room temperature. When the squash is cool enough to handle, use a fork to scrape the inside of the squash, resulting in long spaghetti-like strings. Set aside.

Heat the butter in a large sauté pan over medium heat until it browns lightly, about 5 to 6 minutes. Add the squash and sauté until warm.

Just before serving, add the prepared cilantro pesto and toss through until warm. Garnish with toasted *pepitas*.

Note: *Pepitas* are hulled pumpkin seeds, and while you can find them roasted in most grocery stores, it's simple to do your own. Heat a little olive oil in a skillet; then add the raw *pepitas*. Stir until they're coated with oil and cook until they're fragrant and lightly browned. Remove from the skillet onto a paper towel and then sprinkle with a little sea salt. You can also dust with chile powder or smoked paprika. They keep well in a tightly sealed glass jar and you can use them on salads, soups, or pasta.

Cilantro Pesto Makes 1 cup

This condiment freezes very well and is excellent for dipping breads or livening up a pasta dish. If you have a meat grinder, use it to grind the ingredients. It will give you a nice texture and preserve the color of the cilantro. If you don't have a meat grinder, a food processor is a fine alternative.

¾ cup toasted *pepitas* (p. 48)

1 bunch cilantro, stems included

1 garlic clove

¼ cup blended oil

2 ounces grated Parmesan

Juice of 1 lime

½ teaspoon salt

Pinch of pepper

Run the *pepitas*, cilantro, and garlic through a meat grinder with a fine plate, or process in a food processor until finely chopped. By hand, mix in the oil, Parmesan, lime juice, salt, and pepper.

Use immediately or place in a plastic zipper bag and freeze.

Mesquite Grilled Broccoli with Preserved Lemons and Greek Yogurt Serves 4–6

You might think I'm crazy, but you can do a whole lot more to broccoli than just steam it. I'm still a fan of broccoli covered in cheese sauce, and I can blame my mom for that, but broccoli deserves to take the center stage once in a while. The smoky grill marks in this dish are lightened by preserved lemons and thick Greek yogurt, while fresh mint brings it all to life.

2 pounds broccoli

¼ cup herb oil (page 51)
or blended oil

1 tablespoon coriander seed, crushed

1 tablespoon salt

1 teaspoon pepper

1½ cups plain Greek yogurt

1 clove garlic, chopped

¼ cup rinsed and minced preserved lemons, (recipe follows)

¼ cup fresh mint, chopped

Heat the grill to medium high.

Split the broccoli into 4 to 6 pieces. Using a vegetable peeler, scrape away the first layer of the stem.

Bring a pot of water to a boil and add the broccoli. Cook for 1 minute; then remove to a bowl.

In another bowl, whisk together the oil, coriander, salt, and pepper. Drain the broccoli and toss with the dressing. Place the broccoli on the grill and cook until it has char marks on each side. Remove from the grill to a platter and cover with foil.

In a mixing bowl, combine the yogurt, garlic, preserved lemons, and mint. Pour over the broccoli to serve.

Aromatic Oils

Another way to set yourself apart from all the ordinary cooks out there is to dress up your dishes with aromatic oils. They're simple to make and will keep for weeks in the fridge. Be sure to store them in clean glass bottles with tight-fitting lids.

You've probably noticed the reference to blended oil in many of the recipes in the book. Most of the time, this is my preference for baking, sautéing, and even salad dressings and marinades. It's a combination of 75 percent canola oil and 25 percent olive oil, and it's lightly flavored, has a fairly high smoke point, and is heart-healthy. You can find it at the grocery store, but just make sure you're getting the canola/olive oil blend and not one with lots of other, less healthful options added in.

For herb oil, puree 2 cups of blended oil, 2 cups of fresh basil and ½ cup of fresh parsley in a high-powered blender for one minute. Strain through a mesh strainer lined with coffee filters. This will take several hours.

Oranges and lemons also make flavorful oils for salad dressings or marinades. Simply remove the zest from 3 oranges or 4 lemons, taking care not to include any of the white pith, and cut it into thin strips. Place the strips of zest into a small pan with 2 cups of oil and bring it to a simmer, then remove from the heat and let it cool. The lemon oil benefits from a pinch of turmeric. Strain the zest out and squeeze them to make sure you get as much oil from them as possible, then store in the refrigerator.

Preserved Lemons Makes 1 pint

Preserved lemons last forever. Try these in your favorite jus to give it a punch of flavor!

3 Meyer lemons

1 cup kosher salt

1 tablespoon pickling spice

1 tablespoon sugar

Wash the lemons and cut them into quarters, peels and all. Over a large mixing bowl, smash them with your hands to release the juice.

In a separate bowl, cover the lemons with the salt, pickling spice, and sugar. Mix well.

Pack the lemons into a one-pint Mason jar and cover with the excess juice. Cover with the lid, refrigerate, and let sit for 2 weeks before using.

Roasted Cauliflower with Agave Syrup and Golden Raisins Serves 4–6

Using all of the cauliflower is never a bad thing. Clean off the stems and go for it. Half-inch slices of the entire floret will be caramelized and tender. Just before serving, pick up the browned bits from the pan, creating a glaze with agave nectar and plump golden raisins.

1 head cauliflower

2 tablespoons olive oil

1 tablespoon salt

1 teaspoon pepper

2 tablespoons agave syrup

½ cup golden raisins

1 jalapeño, sliced

½ cup hazelnuts, toasted and crushed

2 tablespoons chives, snipped into ½-inch pieces

Preheat the oven to 400 degrees F.

Slice the cauliflower into ½-inch-thick pieces.

In a large pan, heat the oil over medium heat. Add the cauliflower slices. Brown on both sides. Remove from the pan, season with salt and pepper, and place on a baking sheet.

Add the agave syrup to the pan and cook over medium heat, scraping up any browned bits of cauliflower. When the bottom of the pan is clean, add the golden raisins and jalapeño and stir to coat. Remove from heat and pour the agave sauce over the cauliflower. Place in the oven for 5 to 6 minutes to finish cooking. Remove from the oven.

To serve, garnish with hazelnuts and chives.

Local Vegetable Terrine Serves 4

There is no right or wrong to this madness, so get creative. Start at the local market and see what vegetables inspire you. Ask yourself what flavors will work best together and don't forget to think about robust colors that will create an amazing presentation.

½ cup kosher salt	1 dozen asparagus tips, trimmed to 4 inches
4 baby beets, assorted colors	¼ cup herb oil (page 51) or blended oil
2 zucchini	1 tablespoon salt
2 yellow squash	1 teaspoon pepper
1 small eggplant	1 tablespoon chopped fresh thyme
1 red bell pepper	1 tablespoon chopped fresh oregano
1 yellow bell pepper	1 tablespoon chopped parsley
1 orange bell pepper	Zest of 1 lemon
2 large portobello mushrooms, sliced ¼-inch thick	1 teaspoon minced garlic *(continued)*

Preheat the oven to 350 degrees F.

Place the kosher salt in a baking pan and place the beets on the salt with the skins on. Roast for 1 hour or until tender. Remove from the oven, cool, and peel. Cut into 1-inch cubes.

Preheat the grill to medium high.

Slice the zucchini, yellow squash, and eggplant lengthwise into slices ¼-inch thick. Cut the red, yellow, and orange bell peppers into quarters and remove the seeds. Toss the zucchini, yellow squash, eggplant, bell peppers, portobellos, and asparagus with the herb oil and season with salt and pepper.

Place the vegetables on the grill and cook until tender. Remove from the grill and set aside.

In a small bowl, mix the thyme, oregano, parsley, lemon zest, and garlic. Sprinkle the mixture over the cooked vegetables.

Line a 4 by 8-inch terrine mold with plastic wrap, allowing excess wrap to extend past the sides of the mold. Layer the vegetables in the terrine, being sure to press each layer down evenly. Once the terrine is full, fold the plastic over the top and set the weight on top of the terrine. Place in the refrigerator for at least 24 hours.

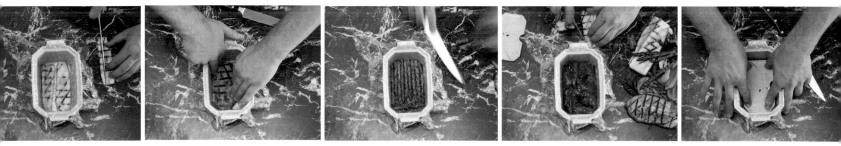

To serve, remove the weight, use the plastic wrap to lift the terrine from the mold, and then remove and discard the plastic wrap. Slice the terrine into 2-inch pieces with a sharp knife. Serve with petite greens and a simple vinaigrette (recipe follows).

Chef's Simple Vinaigrette Makes 2½ cups

It doesn't get much simpler than three ingredients and no seasoning.

¼ cup smooth Dijon mustard

½ cup plus 1 tablespoon champagne vinegar

1½ cups canola oil

Place the mustard and vinegar in the blender and turn on low. While blending, drizzle in the canola oil until emulsified and smooth. Transfer to a bowl and chill.

Arugula Salad Serves 4–6

Arugula and honey are the stars, so treat them that way. Go for the freshest arugula you can find, and while you're at the farmers market, look for the honey people. There's always someone selling local honey. Experiment with different types of honey: mesquite, orange blossom, or jasmine. The bees did some serious business, so let's not disappoint them by using it only to sweeten our morning tea.

2 egg yolks

¼ cup red wine vinegar

¾ cup Dijon mustard

½ cup blended oil

1 cup honey

1 teaspoon salt

½ teaspoon pepper

1 pound arugula

2 pears, sliced

4 ounces blue cheese, crumbled

Add the egg yolks, vinegar, and mustard to the blender and puree until smooth. With the blender running, slowly drizzle in the oil to create an emulsion. Stir in the honey, salt, and pepper.

In a large salad bowl, toss together the arugula and the dressing as desired. Garnish with sliced pears and blue cheese.

Tepary Beans Makes about 5 cups

Tepary beans are one of the oldest crops grown in the desert Southwest and hold a special place in Native culture. Because they're a dryland bean, they take lots of soaking and cooking before they're ready. Once you have them cooked, they can take the place of other beans in chili or soups, and they also make a nice hummus or paté when you grind 'em up.

1 pound white or brown tepary beans

Water to cover

2 tablespoons salt

Spread the dried beans out on a tray and pick through them to get rid of any stones or debris. Wash well, then place in a large bowl. Cover with water and refrigerate for 48 hours. The beans will soak up lots of water, so check to make sure they're still covered and add more water as needed.

After the soaking time, drain the beans and rinse. Add to a large stockpot and cover with water. Bring to a boil and then simmer, uncovered, for several hours until very soft and the starchy taste is gone. If you need to add more water, make sure it's hot so that the beans don't get tough. When the beans are almost cooked, add the salt and continue simmering. The amount of time it takes to cook the beans will vary depending on several factors, so plan for at least six hours and be excited if they cook in less time than that.

Remove the pot from the heat and cool. The beans are now ready to use in other recipes and will keep in the refrigerator for three to five days. They can also be frozen to use later.

Agave-Glazed Heirloom Carrots Serves 6–8

Spring is the best time to find deliciously tender and sweet carrots fresh from the ground. I prefer not to peel my carrots because the skins have a nice earthiness that's too good to toss in the wastebasket. Use the freshest carrots possible because they're going to soak up every bit of flavor you throw at them. If the carrots come with tops, don't be afraid to give them a good wash and toss 'em in at the end. Just warm them through and enjoy.

6 tablespoons unsalted butter

¼ cup peeled and thinly sliced fresh ginger

1 whole garlic clove

3 pounds young carrots, tops removed, washed but not peeled (you can also use regular carrots, peeled and oblique cut)

¼ cup agave syrup

1 cup fresh carrot juice

1½ teaspoons salt

¼ teaspoon freshly ground pepper

In a large skillet, melt the butter. Add the ginger and garlic. Cook over medium heat until fragrant, about 2 minutes. Add the carrots and agave syrup and cook over moderately high heat, stirring occasionally, until the carrots are lightly browned, about 6 minutes. Add the carrot juice and bring to a simmer. Season with salt and pepper. Cover and cook the carrots over low heat until tender, about 8 minutes. Uncover and cook over moderate heat until the carrots are glazed, about 5 minutes longer. Remove from heat and discard the ginger and garlic.

Grilled Artichokes with Poblano-Truffle Aioli Serves 4–6

Artichokes aren't as scary as you think, but be careful. I've lost a few times when going one-on-one with a spiny artichoke, but they're too good to let the spiky leaves stop you. Steaming first will not only tenderize them but also infuse them with flavor. Then hit the grill for some char that pairs up nicely with the poblano-truffle aioli. Earthiness at its prime.

1½ cups Garlic Aioli (page 102) or mayo

1 teaspoon sherry vinegar

4 cloves roasted garlic (recipe follows)

⅛ teaspoon truffle oil, or to taste

2 poblanos, roasted, peeled, seeded, and chopped

2 lemons, halved

3 fresh bay leaves

2 raw garlic cloves

4 baby artichokes

Make the poblano-truffle aioli by combining the Garlic Aioli or mayonnaise, sherry vinegar, roasted garlic, truffle oil, and poblanos in a blender. Puree and then chill.

Fill a large pot with 2 to 3 inches of water and add the lemons, bay leaves, and raw garlic cloves. Fit with a steamer basket and bring to a simmer.

Wash the artichokes and use a pair of kitchen shears to cut off the thorny ends of the artichoke leaves. Slice about 1 inch off the top of each artichoke. Remove the tough small leaves at the bottom and peel the stem with a vegetable peeler. Cut each artichoke in half lengthwise, exposing the hearts. Use a spoon to scrape out the fuzzy choke.

Place the artichokes in the steamer basket and cover. Cook for 25 to 35 minutes, or until tender. While they're steaming, heat the grill to medium high.

Remove the artichokes from the heat and grill for a few minutes to add some char. Remove and serve with aioli for dipping.

Roasted Garlic Makes 1 cup

I use roasted garlic in many of my recipes, so I always have it on hand. The slow cooking of the garlic cloves transforms the flavors from assertive and harsh into delicate and slightly sweet. Enjoy this garlic as a spread or substitute for chopped garlic. And of course, the reserved oil will be perfumed with garlic flavor, which means it's time to grab some bread.

1 cup garlic cloves, peeled

2 cups blended oil

Place the garlic and the oil in a saucepan over medium heat. Bring to a simmer and reduce the heat to low. Simmer 25 to 30 minutes until the garlic is soft and tender. Remove from heat.

Cool in the oil and then strain. Store the garlic in an airtight container in the refrigerator. Reserve the oil, if desired.

OCEANFRONT PROPERTY

When I think of Southwestern cuisine, I don't typically include California, and most Texans are doing their own thing with food. So why am I including seafood? That's easy. We're close to two coasts, the Pacific Coast of California and the coast of the Sea of Cortez in Mexico. I source things like Santa Barbara mussels and California halibut from the Pacific, and fresh Gulf shrimp and hand-caught *cabrilla*, a type of sea bass, from Mexico. When you're buying seafood, it's important to make sure you're choosing sustainable varieties. Let's look at different types of seafood, unique ways to cook it, and easy family-style preparations. Throw out a line and we'll cook up today's fresh catch.

Grilled Gulf Shrimp with Spicy Cocktail Sauce Serves 6–8

These decadent, smoky, grilled shrimp are phenomenal when paired with spiced-up cocktail sauce. The pearls of horseradish are designed to pop in your mouth and give you that sinus-clearing bang. Source fresh shrimp if possible, but if not, go for ones that are natural and haven't been pumped with fillers. It's all about the shrimp.

1 quart grape seed oil

3 tablespoons blended oil

1 tablespoon chile powder

1 tablespoon paprika

1 teaspoon oregano

1 teaspoon salt

¼ teaspoon pepper

3 pounds fresh jumbo shrimp, peeled and deveined

2 cups ketchup

2 lemons, juice and zest

4 teaspoons prepared horseradish

2 teaspoons Worcestershire sauce

2 dashes of Tabasco sauce

3 jars (8-ounce) prepared horseradish

7 ounces water

1 tablespoon agar-agar (page 17)

1 lime, juice and zest

2 tablespoons finely chopped cilantro

Refrigerate the grape seed oil overnight.

In a large bowl, whisk together the 3 tablespoons of blended oil, chile powder, paprika, oregano, salt, and pepper. Add the shrimp and toss to coat. Refrigerate for 1 to 2 hours.

To make the cocktail sauce, in a small bowl, mix the ketchup, lemon juice and zest, 4 teaspoons horseradish, Worcestershire sauce, and Tabasco until smooth. Refrigerate.

Press the 8-ounce jars of prepared horseradish through a fine strainer to get 7 ounces of horseradish juice. Puree the juice with the water and agar-agar until smooth. Place in a squeeze bottle with a fine tip.

Remove the chilled grapeseed oil from the refrigerator. Squeeze small drops of the horseradish mixture into the oil, creating tiny spheres of horseradish that should solidify instantly. Let sit for at least 10 minutes, then strain the horseradish spheres out of the oil and use to garnish the top of the cocktail sauce. The oil can be saved and used again.

Heat the grill to medium-high. Add the shrimp and cook 2 minutes on each side. Remove from heat and toss with the lime juice and zest and cilantro. Refrigerate until chilled.

Pile the shrimp high and serve with the cocktail sauce on the side.

Pan-Seared Sea Bass with Sweet Corn Broth Serves 4

This dish can be done in one large sauté pan. That's always a plus for me because I don't like leaving a ton of dishes for the dishwasher. Buy a whole fish and have the butcher remove the fillets for you, and be sure to ask for the bones to make stock. This is best in the summer because you need creamy sweet corn with kernels bursting with juice to give you that milky broth. The light sauce is balanced by the crispy skin of the sea bass. Served with some sautéed greens on the side, it makes a delightful and comfy summer dinner.

Sweet Corn Broth

2 tablespoons blended oil

1 small leek, white part only, cleaned and diced

1 clove garlic, sliced

2 ears of sweet white corn, kernels removed, cobs cut into thirds

2 teaspoons ground cumin

¼ teaspoon turmeric

½ cup dry white wine

1 cup seafood stock (recipe follows) or dark vegetable stock (page 44)

1 cup water

¼ cup thinly sliced russet potato

4 tablespoons unsalted butter, cut in pieces

1 teaspoon salt

½ teaspoon pepper

Fish

1 whole sea bass (3 to 4 pound)

1 teaspoon salt

¼ teaspoon pepper

4 tablespoons blended oil

(continued)

Sweet Corn Broth: In a large sauté pan, heat the oil and sauté the leek until tender. Add the garlic and corn kernels and sauté another 2 minutes. Stir in the cumin and turmeric and toast in the pan 30–40 seconds. Pour in the white wine, stock, and water. Add the corncobs and bring to a simmer. Once simmering, add the russet potatoes and simmer for 15 to 20 minutes. Remove from heat, remove the corncobs and discard them. Let cool slightly. Puree the corn sauce in the blender, and while pureeing, add the butter. Strain through several layers of cheesecloth, squeezing at the end to get all of the liquid out. Add the salt and pepper and adjust to taste. Set the sauce aside and keep warm.

Fish: Cut each fillet into 2 pieces and score the skin side with 1- to 2-inch slices just through the skin. Season each side with the salt and pepper.

Add the blended oil to the same sauté pan and heat. When the oil shimmers, add the fillets, skin side down. Apply pressure to the fillets with a fish spatula for the first 30 seconds, ensuring the entire skin has contact with the pan and does not curl up. Once the skin is crispy and browned (3 to 4 minutes), flip the fish to finish cooking an additional 3 minutes. Remove from heat and serve with the sauce.

How to Find Sustainable Seafood

As people have become fonder of fish and seafood, the demand for some species has driven them almost to the point of extinction. Orange roughy, red snapper, and others are almost non-existent in the wild. Not only that, but some fishing methods, like longlines and gillnets, have a tendency to catch other species that might be endangered, so when you eat a fish like ahi tuna that was caught on a longline, you might be contributing to the demise of sea turtles, sharks, or sea birds. And then there's the issue of farming. Many farmed fish, like salmon, create an environmental disaster in the fisheries around them. Oysters and mussels, on the other hand, are perfectly acceptable when they come from farmed operations. That's why it's important to know what kind of fish to buy, and why it's so important to buy from a reputable fishmonger.

It's a complicated subject, but the Monterey Bay Aquarium has made the process of buying fish and seafood a little easier. Their Seafood Watch program tells you which fish to avoid and which are good replacements. The cool thing is that they've developed an app for your smart phone, so when you go to the grocery store, you can look up the information on the spot. www.montereybayaquarium.org

Seafood Stock Makes 1 gallon

This stock is the ideal base for chowders or *cioppino*. Ask your fishmonger or butcher for bones. Sometimes they're free.

5 pounds flat fish bones

1 cup dry white wine

½ cup sliced leeks

½ cup sliced fennel

½ cup diced onion

¼ cup sliced mushrooms

4 peppercorns

1 bay leaf

3 quarts water

½ pound Santa Barbara mussels

Remove any fins, tails, heads, or skin from the fish bones and rinse well in cold water.

In a small pan over medium heat, reduce the white wine by half.

Place the bones, leeks, fennel, onions, mushrooms, peppercorns, and bay leaf into an 8-quart stockpot. Add the wine and water. Bring to a simmer for 30 minutes, skimming off any impurities that rise to the top.

Add the mussels and simmer an additional 5 minutes. Remove from heat and allow to sit for 15 minutes to allow the particles in the stock to settle at the bottom. Use a ladle to remove the stock from the top, leaving the sediment on the bottom to discard. Strain and cool.

Freeze for up to 2 months or refrigerate for use within 4 days.

California Halibut with Sautéed Succotash Serves 4–6

Alaskan halibut is one of my favorites, but the price seems to get higher every year. A great alternative is the California halibut, a smaller fish also from the Pacific coast. Don't be afraid to ask your local fishmonger to order this for you if they don't have it. They are happy to bring in specialty fish, and you know it will be its freshest since you're the reason it's making the trip.

Fish

4 California halibut fillets (6-ounce)

1 tablespoon salt

1 teaspoon pepper

¼ cup blended oil

Succotash

¼ cup blended oil

2 tablespoons butter

½ cup fava beans, blanched

**2 ears fresh corn,
kernels scraped from the cobs**

1 cup zucchini, diced

1 red bell pepper, diced

¼ cup red onion, diced

¼ cup diced poblano

1 jalapeño, minced

2 cups wild arugula

Fish: Season the fillets with salt and pepper.

Heat a large sauté pan over high heat and add ¼ cup of oil. When the oil shimmers, add the fish to the pan. Sauté for 2 to 3 minutes until they begin to loosen from the pan on their own. Once they have a nice golden color on the bottom, reduce the heat to medium and let the fish continue to cook 4 to 5 minutes longer. Flip the fish over, remove from heat, and let rest in the pan another 4 to 5 minutes.

Succotash: In another large sauté pan, heat the oil with the butter until shimmering. Add the beans, corn, zucchini, red bell pepper, onion, poblano, and jalapeño and cook until tender, 6 to 7 minutes. Fold in the arugula during the last few seconds of cooking.

Serve the fish over a bed of succotash.

Seared Scallops with Meyer Lemon Curd Serves 4

If you're going to cook scallops, always source the dry-packed diver scallops, which are sustainably harvested and packaged without additives. Frozen scallops just won't give you that crispy golden crust. Rest them on a few sheets of cheesecloth for 10 to 15 minutes before you sear them. This will dry the outside nicely and create a perfect surface for searing. We're going to pair the scallops with a sweet and tart Meyer lemon curd. Meyer lemons are a cross between a true lemon and a mandarin orange, and they have a unique flavor with a sweetness unlike any other lemon. Then we're going to lighten things up with some whipped cream.

1 dozen large, dry-packed diver scallops

2 teaspoons salt

¼ teaspoon pepper

¼ cup blended oil

2 tablespoons butter

1 garlic bulb, halved

2 sprigs thyme

1 tablespoon hibiscus powder

2 cups Meyer lemon curd (page 72)

Season the scallops with salt and pepper.

Heat a sauté pan and add the oil. When the oil shimmers, add the scallops. Sauté until golden brown on one side, then flip and add the butter, garlic, and thyme to the pan. As the butter begins to foam, spoon it over the scallops for an additional 2 minutes. Remove the scallops from the heat and lightly dust them with the hibiscus powder.

Serve with a large dollop of Meyer lemon curd on the side.

Meyer Lemon Curd Makes 2½ cups

Lemon curd isn't just for pie. Try it here with sweet and luscious scallops or even paired with grilled asparagus and crispy onions.

3 egg yolks

½ cup sugar

Juice and zest of 2 Meyer lemons

2 tablespoons cold unsalted butter, cut into cubes

1 cup heavy whipping cream

In the top of a double boiler, whisk the egg yolks and sugar for about 2 minutes until smooth. Whisk in the lemon juice and zest until combined.

Bring several inches of water to a simmer in the bottom of the double boiler and place the pan on top, making sure that the water doesn't touch the bottom. Stir the mixture constantly with a rubber spatula until it begins to thicken, about 7 to 10 minutes. Remove from heat.

Whisk in the butter, one cube at a time.

Cover by placing plastic wrap directly on the surface of the curd and then refrigerate. When the curd has cooled completely, whip the heavy cream to soft peaks. Remove one cup of lemon curd and fold the whipped cream into it.

Refrigerate any extra curd for up to a week and use it on toast or scones for breakfast.

Smoked Salmon Croquettes with Chipotle Aioli Makes 2 dozen

This dish is a great way to use trimmings from center-cut salmon fillets. Or save a buck or two a pound and ask the butcher for any trimmings left over from that day's salmon. Those lonely salmon scraps are going to be happy you found them when they end up salt-cured, mesquite-smoked, and crispy fried to perfection.

Smoked Salmon
2 pounds salmon belly or fillet

1½ tablespoons salt

Croquettes
1 poblano pepper, roasted, peeled, and seeded

1 red bell pepper, roasted, peeled, and seeded

1 red onion, roasted and cut into ¼-inch dice

1 cup Garlic Aioli (page 102) or mayonnaise

1 tablespoon Dijon mustard

½ lemon, juice and zest

⅓ cup parsley, chopped

2 teaspoons salt

½ teaspoon pepper

3 eggs

3 to 4 cups panko bread crumbs

1 quart oil, for frying

Chipotle Aioli
1 cup Garlic Aioli (page 102) or mayonnaise

⅓ can (7-ounce) chipotles in adobo

½ lemon, juice and zest

1 teaspoon water

¼ cup honey

¼ teaspoon salt

Smoked Salmon: Cover the salmon in 1½ tablespoons salt and refrigerate overnight.

Heat a smoker and allow the salmon to smoke for about 10 minutes, stirring occasionally. Remove from the smoker and cool. If you prefer, you could use The Smoking Gun, but the smoke flavor will be significantly less.

Croquettes: Puree the poblano, red bell pepper, and red onion in the blender. In a medium bowl, mix together the puree, parsley, salmon, aioli or mayonnaise, mustard, salt, pepper, eggs, and panko. You may need to adjust the mixture with more panko. It should be moist, but still hold together. Season with salt and pepper. Form into balls about the size of golf balls.

In a deep saucepot, heat 1 quart of oil to 350 degrees F and fry the croquettes until golden brown. Remove from oil and drain on paper towels. Season with salt immediately.

Chipotle Aioli: Place the aioli or mayonnaise, chipotles, lemon juice and zest, water, honey, and salt in a blender and process until smooth.

Serve the croquettes with the sauce on the side.

Blue Corn Fried Oysters with Kumquat Gastrique Serves 2

These oysters rock! I use Gulf oysters, but any large, plump oyster will work. Ask your supplier to shuck these for you ahead of time and leave them in the oyster liquor. This will save you time and you can get right to eating. The light blue corn flour dust has an herbaceous quality that gives the oysters character. Dunk and dip these bad boys in a tangy and sweet kumquat gastrique.

Oysters

12 Gulf oysters, shucked

1 cup buttermilk

2 cups blue corn flour

1 quart blended oil

1 teaspoon salt

Kumquat Gastrique

12 kumquats, halved and seeded, juice reserved

1 jalapeño, seeded and sliced

1 cup citrus or rice wine vinegar

1 cup light corn syrup

½ teaspoon salt

¼ teaspoon pepper

Oysters: Soak the oysters in buttermilk for 10–15 minutes. Drain and toss the oysters with the blue corn flour until evenly coated.

In a large saucepan, heat the oil to 320 to 330 degrees F. Add the oysters one at a time and fry until golden brown and crispy. Remove from the oil and drain on paper towels. Sprinkle with salt.

Kumquat Gastrique: Place the kumquats and their juice, the jalapeño, vinegar, corn syrup, and salt and pepper in a skillet over medium-high heat and simmer until the kumquats are tender, about 5 to 10 minutes. Remove from heat and serve immediately with the oysters.

You might wonder why anyone would want to eat such a forbidding-looking plant. It's covered in spines and it seems like they jump into your clothes and skin even when you just walk by. But really, the prickly pear has much to offer from a flavor standpoint as well as nutritionally. They're packed with vitamins, low in calories, and can even help control diabetes and cholesterol.

So how do you get past the prickly exterior and get to the good stuff?

In the spring, the cactus puts out new shoots, and these can be harvested when they're tender and about the size of your hand. They're called nopales, and once you clean them, they can be grilled, sautéed, dried, or pickled. When sliced into thin strips, they're called nopalitos. To clean them, hold the tough stem end with a pair of tongs and scrape the surface of the nopal with a sharp knife. Go against the growth of the spines and scrape them all off on both sides. Then cut a thin slice off from around the edge—you won't be able to get all of the thorns off of the edge, and you don't want them in your tongue. Cut off the stem end, rinse the nopal, and you're ready to go. When they're fresh they can have a slimy consistency, but cooking will get rid of it and leave behind just crunchy goodness.

The fruit appears in the fall, and you have to get to them before the wildlife does. One note—it's illegal in many places to harvest any type of cactus on public lands, so you can do this only if you have them in your own yard or know someone who does. Use a pair of tongs to pull the red fruit from the plants. If it's ripe, it should come right off. Place the fruit into a bucket and when your harvest is complete, take them to the sink. Hold each piece of fruit with the tongs and scrub it with a vegetable brush. Rinse it well under running water.

To make prickly pear juice or puree, place the cleaned fruit into a large saucepan and cover with water. Bring the pot to a boil over high heat and then reduce heat to simmer for about 5 minutes. Cool slightly, and then add the fruit to the blender and puree. Strain though cheesecloth or a fine mesh strainer. Four cups of picked fruit will give you about one cup of juice. At this point you can refrigerate or freeze it to use in drinks, make syrup, or experiment.

You'll probably end up with some pesky little stickers in your fingers, but if you rinse your hands with lemon juice or another acid, like vinegar, they'll disappear.

Mussels with Nopales Serves 2

Some of the best mussels come from California. Since mussels are harvested year round, they can vary in size. I go for the big ones because they're juicy and cook up plump with flavor. Don't get caught up in the old wives' tale that says if a mussel doesn't open when you cook it, it's bad. Open it yourself, give it a smell, and look at it. You'll know. No mussels left behind.

2 fresh *nopales*, or ½ cup canned *nopales*

2 ounces blended oil

2 cloves garlic, smashed

½ onion, chopped

1 tablespoon butter

¼ cup chorizo pork belly, small dice (page 113) or bacon, sliced into *lardons*

3 to 4 cloves garlic, chopped

1 pound fresh Santa Barbara mussels, scrubbed and rinsed

½ cup chardonnay or other dry white wine

½ cup Smoked Paprika Coulis (recipe follows)

1 teaspoon salt

Pinch of pepper

¼ cup cilantro, chopped

Clean the fresh *nopales* (page 75) and cut into thin strips *(nopalitos)*. Add blended oil and heat over medium heat. Place in a small pan over medium heat and add the garlic and onion. If using canned *nopales*, drain, chop, and add to the pan with the garlic and onion. Cook for about 10 minutes, stirring frequently. Strain and cool.

In a large pan over medium-high heat, sauté the pork belly in the butter until the belly begins to caramelize, 4 to 5 minutes. Add the garlic and sauté another 2 to 3 minutes. Add the mussels, white wine, *nopalitos*, and smoked paprika coulis. Cover and bring to a simmer. Stir the mussels to evenly coat with the sauce. Simmer covered for 4 to 5 minutes until the mussels open and are fully cooked. Remove from heat. Season with salt and pepper.

Serve immediately in large bowls and pour the sauce over. Garnish with chopped cilantro.

Smoked Paprika Coulis Makes 1 quart

This sauce pairs well with seafood and poultry and adds a bit of smokiness to any dish. Some canned tomatoes can be very salty, so taste before you season.

4 tablespoons blended oil

1 red bell pepper, chopped

½ onion, chopped

5 cloves roasted garlic (page 62)

1 can (28-ounce) San Marzano tomatoes

2 cups dark vegetable stock (page 44) or water

1 tablespoon smoked sweet paprika

Salt

Pepper

Heat the oil in a large sauté pan over medium-high heat. When it simmers, add the red pepper and onion and sauté until tender, about 5 minutes. Add the garlic, canned tomatoes, and stock. Stir in the paprika and salt and pepper to taste. Simmer for 15 minutes. Remove from heat, cool slightly, and puree.

Cool completely, then store in an airtight container in the refrigerator for up to 3 days, or freeze in small batches for up to 1 month.

Whole Roasted Tuna Loin Serves 6–8

Call this in to your butcher in advance (and be sure to ask if the tuna was caught by troll or pole and line, instead of by purse seining or longlines). You want a three- to three-and-a-half-pound bread loaf cut of ahi tuna. That's the good stuff—center cut, no bloodline, no skin, just melt-in-your-mouth awesomeness. This recipe is unique because it can be served warm immediately with a tamari butter sauce or cold with pickled carrots and jicama. Either way, the smoky cumin and pops of citrus will amaze you. The secret to the deep flavor in this dish is the sear. Make sure you let the surface get golden brown and be sure to pick up all the bits from the pan with a squeeze of citrus juice.

3 pounds ahi tuna, bread loaf cut

2 teaspoons salt

½ teaspoon pepper

4 tablespoons blended oil

1 lemon, zest coarsely grated and juice

1 lime, zest coarsely grated and juice

1 orange, zest coarsely grated and juice

½ teaspoon ground coriander

½ teaspoon ground cardamom

½ teaspoon ground annatto

1 teaspoon ground cumin

1 teaspoon cayenne

Season the tuna with salt and pepper. Heat the oil in a large pan and add the tuna, searing on all sides until golden brown. Remove the tuna from the pan and set aside.

Over medium heat, pour the lemon, lime, and orange juices into the pan and scrape up all the bits from cooking the tuna. Add the lemon, lime, and orange zest. Stir in the coriander, cardamom, annatto, cumin, and cayenne. Remove from heat, cool slightly, and rub the resulting mixture into the tuna loin. Place in the refrigerator for 30 minutes.

Heat oven to 400 degrees F.

Place the tuna on a roasting rack and place in the oven for 8 to 10 minutes. Remove from the oven, let rest 5 minutes, and then slice into 1-inch-thick pieces.

Chef's Southwestern Cioppino Serves 8

A little bit of this, a little bit of that—it's all good as long as it's fresh. The next time you hit the supermarket or fish market, see what's available and what's at its peak. I like to have a variety: some shellfish, a delicate white fish, and thick chunks of fatty salmon. The foundation is a great broth.

4 tablespoons blended oil

½ onion, sliced

½ poblano, sliced

½ red bell pepper, sliced

½ yellow bell pepper, sliced

6 garlic cloves, smashed

1 cup dry white wine, divided

2 cups seafood stock (page 68)
or low sodium clam juice

1 cup Smoked Paprika Coulis (page 77)

¾ cup grape seed oil, divided

1 pound jumbo shrimp, deveined with the shell on

1 pound Alaskan or California halibut, cut into 1-inch cubes

4 fillets wild salmon (2 ounces each)

½ pound Santa Barbara mussels, scrubbed and cleaned

½ pound jumbo lump crab meat

1 dozen Spanish olives, halved

2 tablespoons capers, rinsed (optional)

2 tablespoons Cilantro Pesto (page 49)

1 tablespoon salt

1 teaspoon pepper

(continued)

Heat the oil in a large saucepot over medium-high heat. Add the onion, poblano, and red and yellow bell peppers and sauté until tender, 5 to 6 minutes. Add the garlic and sauté an additional 3 minutes. Add ½ cup white wine and cook until reduced by half. Add the seafood stock and coulis. Reduce heat and simmer for 15 minutes.

Meanwhile, in a large sauté pan, heat ¼ cup of the grape seed oil and sauté the shrimp until barely pink. Remove from the pan and set aside to rest. Repeat separately with the remaining grape seed oil for the halibut and salmon, creating a golden brown crust on each side without cooking all the way through. Remove them from the pans to rest.

Add the remaining white wine to the pan and cook while scraping up all the little browned bits. When the bottom of the pan is deglazed, add the contents of the pan to the seafood broth.

Add the mussels to the broth and simmer for 3 minutes. Add the salmon, halibut, and shrimp and cook an additional 3 to 4 minutes until all of the seafood is cooked through.

Finish the cioppino by stirring in the jumbo lump crab meat, Spanish olives, capers, cilantro pesto, salt and pepper.

Serve immediately over a bed of saffron rice or boiled lentils.

Crab Mashed Avocado with Pickled Scallions Serves 4–6

If you're going to make the effort to put crab into mashed avocado, make sure you go fresh. Most crab legs in the store have been frozen in advance, so look for already picked crab meat. It will be labeled fresh and non-pasteurized, and yes, it's expensive. I like to use jumbo lump crab, but as long as it's fresh, any grade will do.

Pickled Scallions

1 cup water

1 cup cider vinegar

2 tablespoons sugar

Pinch of salt

4 scallions, cut into ¼-inch pieces

Dip

3 avocados

½ pound lump crab

Juice of 1 lime

1 teaspoon salt

⅛ teaspoon cayenne

2 kiwis, peeled and minced

Tortilla chips

Pickled Scallions: In a small saucepan over medium-high heat, bring the water, cider vinegar, sugar, and salt to a boil. Add the scallions. Remove from heat and let cool completely at room temperature.

Dip: Peel and seed the avocados and then mash in a mixing bowl until smooth. Add the crab, lime juice, salt, cayenne, and kiwis. Mix well.

Strain the scallions and fold them into the avocado/crab mix.

Chill or enjoy immediately with homemade tortilla chips.

BIRDS

Poultry is one of my favorite proteins to cook. It can be prepared in many ways and takes on other flavors well. The meat can be flavorful and tender, and the lean cuts of breast balance with the dark, fattier leg meat. And when I talk about poultry, I'm not referring to just chicken. The Southwest is home to many birds and is a bountiful area for hunting. Turkeys, quail, dove, and even ostrich thrive in the desert landscape, and you can find them on many menus around these parts. Some game birds may be hard to source at a local grocery store, but there are many websites that will ship you cleaned and frozen game meat at an affordable price. Some may not be your go-to dinner, but they will surprise and impress your guests.

Baked Chicken Drums Serves 4–6

When you're going to cook for a large number of people, this recipe is the best because you can easily scale it up to serve 10 to 20 hungry partiers. Slow-roasted chicken drums have a ton of flavor and are especially good with sauces. The sweet-tangy sauce uses fresh prickly pear fruit and salty tamari. Adding the ginger gives it a nice spice and gets the Southwestern-Asian fusion flowing.

4 pounds chicken drumsticks

1 gallon Chef's Brine (recipe follows)

½ cup orange oil (page 51) or blended oil

1 tablespoon salt

1 teaspoon pepper

1 cup fresh prickly pear juice

4 tablespoons brown sugar

2 cloves garlic

2 tablespoons tamari

2 tablespoons mirin

½ teaspoon sesame oil

1 teaspoon minced serrano pepper

¾ teaspoon xanthan gum (see note)

1 tablespoon sesame seeds, toasted

1 tablespoon sliced scallion

Submerge the drumsticks in the brine and refrigerate for 1½ hours.

Preheat the oven to 375 degrees F and put a large roasting pan inside to heat.

Remove the drumsticks from the brine and pat them dry. Coat with the orange oil and lightly season with salt and pepper. Place in the pre-heated roasting pan and bake for 25 to 28 minutes until cooked through. When you poke a knife through the thickest part of the drum, the juices should run clear.

Meanwhile, place the prickly pear juice, brown sugar, garlic, tamari, mirin, sesame oil, and serrano into a blender and puree until smooth. Add the xanthan gum toward the end to thicken the sauce until it coats the back of a spoon.

Once the chicken drums are finished cooking, remove them from the oven and pour the prickly pear glaze over. The pan should be warm enough to heat the sauce and glaze the chicken. If it is not and the sauce is still runny, return the pan to the oven for a few minutes to reduce and glaze.

Garnish with toasted sesame seeds and scallions.

Note: Xanthan gum is an emulsifier and thickener derived from fermented corn sugar. It has become popular in gluten-free baking to bind the flours together, so it's easy to find in the gluten-free baking section in your grocery store.

Brining Times

Soaking in brine adds moisture and flavor to your favorite meats. Be sure to use a big enough container, make sure the meat is completely submerged, and keep it refrigerated.

ITEM	BRINE TIME
Whole chicken (4–5 Pounds)	8–12 hours
Chicken parts	1½ hours
Chicken breasts	1 hour
Whole turkey	24–48 hours
Turkey breast	5–10 hours
Cornish game hens	2 hours
Shrimp	30 minutes
Pork chops	12–24 hours
Pork tenderloin (whole)	12–24 hours

Chef's Brine Makes 1 gallon

This brine will enhance the flavor and moisture of almost anything, from a whole chicken to a pork loin or a roasting ham. It takes a little extra time, but the difference is well worth it.

1 gallon water

1 cup kosher salt

⅓ cup sugar

6 bay leaves

½ cup garlic cloves, smashed

2 lemons, juice and zest

1 bunch parsley, shredded

Add the water, salt, sugar, bay leaves, garlic, lemon juice and zest, and parsley to a large stockpot. Bring to a boil over high heat and cook until the sugar and salt have dissolved.

Cool completely before using.

Basic Boiled Spanish Rice Serves 6

I'm a sucker for starches and this one satisfies every time. Try adding some jalapeño powder to spice it up.

¾ pound chorizo (page 114)

1 small onion, finely diced

1 clove garlic, sliced

1½ cups basmati rice

3¼ cups chicken stock (page 95) or dark vegetable stock (page 44)

1 teaspoon salt

¼ teaspoon pepper

12 large pimento-stuffed olives

2 tablespoons chopped cilantro

Sauté the chorizo in a large pan over medium heat until completely rendered. Add the onions and sauté until tender, about 4–5 minutes. Add the garlic and sauté an additional 2 minutes. Add the rice and let it toast in the pork fat for 2–3 minutes. Add the stock, salt, and pepper. Bring to a simmer. Cover and let cook over low heat for 15 to 18 minutes until the rice is tender. Remove from the heat and fold in the olives and cilantro. Adjust the salt and pepper, if needed.

Roasted Quail with Chorizo Stuffing Serves 6

Quail is one of my favorite birds, and I always have them in my freezer. With a stuffing of homemade cho-rizo and roasted peppers, this becomes a decadent treat. If you want to go your own way, try mixing other flavors into the stuffing. I would suggest smoky bacon and apples in place of the chorizo and peppers. It's all good.

1 poblano

1 jalapeño

2 scallions

2 tablespoons blended oil

½ pound chorizo sausage (page 114)

½ onion, minced

1 cup chicken stock (page 95)

⅛ teaspoon ground cumin

2 tablespoons masa harina (see note on page 89)

½ teaspoon salt

⅛ teaspoon pepper

Juice of ½ lime

1 tablespoon fresh chopped cilantro

Canola oil, for oiling the birds

6 quail (4–5 ounces each), cleaned

Heat the grill to medium high.

Roast the poblano and jalapeño until blackened all over and the scallions until charred. Place the poblano and jalapeño in a bowl and cover with plastic wrap. Allow to steam for 15 minutes. Slice the grilled scallions. Peel and seed the poblano and jalapeño, and then dice. Set aside.

In a sauté pan, heat the oil until shimmering and add the chorizo. Let the chorizo cook through and release its oils and color. Add the onion and sauté until tender. Add the chicken stock, roasted poblano and jalapeño, scallions, and cumin. Bring to a simmer, quickly whisk in the masa harina, and then switch to a wooden spoon for stirring. Stir frequently over low heat for 15 to 18 minutes until thick. Stir in the salt and pepper, lime juice, and cilantro. Remove from heat and transfer to a plate to cool to room temperature.

When cool, divide the stuffing into 6 equal portions of about ⅓ cup each. Place the stuffing inside the cavity of each quail and use butcher's twine to truss the legs.

Lightly spray the quail with canola oil and season the outside with salt and pepper. Chill until completely cold, about 15 minutes.

Meanwhile, heat the grill to medium high.

Remove the quail from the refrigerator and place on the grill. Cook until each side is golden brown. Cover the grill and cook an additional 6 minutes until the stuffing is warmed through.

Serve with Basic Boiled Spanish Rice (page 87).

Note: Masa harina is corn flour used to make the dough for tamales and corn tortillas. You can find it in most grocery stores.

Cast Iron Turducken Serves 6–8

Patience, my friend. This recipe takes lots of time and love, but it's worth every minute. Start several days in advance—I've broken out the steps for each ingredient. Cast iron turducken takes all of the lovely traditional turducken flavors and transforms them with a Southwestern twist: Turkey becomes turkey *confit* and then *machaca*. Chicken becomes chicken chorizo. And duck is represented by *foie gras* butter and duck fat, which you can order at the butcher shop. Take this to your next family holiday party and people will ignore Aunt Sandy's dried-out ham.

Turkey Confit Machaca

4 turkey legs, about 2 pounds

¼ cup cumin seeds, toasted and crushed

1 ounce Chef's Basic Cure (page 39)

2 quarts duck fat

½ red onion, finely diced

½ jalapeño, minced

½ red bell pepper, finely diced

1 tablespoon ground cumin

1 tablespoon smoked sweet paprika

2 limes, juice and zest

½ cup cilantro, chopped

2 cups chicken stock (page 95)

Chicken Chorizo

1 pound boneless chicken thighs,
or 1 pound ground chicken

½ teaspoon cayenne

1 teaspoon smoked hot paprika

½ teaspoon annatto, ground

¼ teaspoon chile pepper flakes

2 tablespoons sherry vinegar
or cider vinegar

1 tablespoon salt

¼ teaspoon pepper

3 cloves garlic

The Turducken

1 quart chicken stock

2 ounces blended oil

½ cup shallots, minced

1 tablespoon minced garlic

1 cup white wine

2 cups cooked tepary beans (page 57)

2 jalapeños, sliced

1 bunch asparagus, ends trimmed,
cut into 1½-inch pieces

¼ cup *foie gras* butter (recipe follows)

1 teaspoon salt

½ teaspoon pepper *(continued)*

Turkey Confit Machaca: Rub the turkey legs with the cumin and dry cure. Place the legs in a 1-gallon plastic zipper bag for 3 days, turning over every day and distributing the liquid. After 3 days, remove the legs from the bag, rinse off the liquid, and place in the refrigerator on a kitchen towel and let air dry for at least 4 hours.

Preheat the oven to 190 degrees F.

In a small saucepan, warm the duck fat until melted. Place the turkey legs in a large heavy-bottomed pot. Pour the duck fat over the turkey legs until they're covered. Place in the oven and cook at a very low simmer for 8 hours. Remove from the oven and let cool to room temperature. The turkey meat should fall from the bones and be exceedingly tender. Remove the turkey from the bone. Discard bones and skin.

In a large stockpot, simmer the turkey meat, red onion, jalapeño, red bell pepper, cumin, paprika, lime juice and zest, cilantro, and chicken stock. Reduce until the liquid has completely evaporated. Remove from the heat and refrigerate until ready to use.

Chicken Chorizo: Grind together the chicken thighs, cayenne, paprika, annatto, chile pepper flakes, vinegar, salt, pepper, and garlic. Cover and chill one hour. If you're using ground chicken, mince the garlic and then combine all of the ingredients by hand. Refrigerate until ready to assemble the turducken.

The Turducken: Bring the chicken stock to a boil in a saucepot and cook until reduced by half. Remove from heat and set aside.

Heat a large cast iron pot and add the blended oil. Add the shallots and garlic and cook for 2–3 minutes until tender. Add the chicken chorizo and sauté until the meat is cooked and resembles cooked ground beef, 6 to 8 minutes. Add the white wine and simmer for 5 minutes. Add the turkey *machaca*, tepary beans, jalapeños, and reduced chicken stock. Simmer for 10 minutes. Fold in the asparagus and *foie gras* butter, add the salt and pepper and taste to adjust the seasoning, if necessary. Remove from the heat and serve from the pot with a rustic grilled bread loaf for dipping.

Foie Gras Butter Makes 1 pound

This decadent butter is delectable to finish sauces, risottos, and stews. Even as a spread for rustic country bread, it will liven up the party.

½ **pound unsalted butter**

½ **pound** *foie gras* **scraps, cleaned**

1 teaspoon salt

1 teaspoon fresh thyme leaves, coarsely chopped

1 tablespoon brandy

Let the butter and *foie gras* come to room temperature.

Using a standing mixer with a paddle, whip the *foie gras* and butter on medium-high speed until smooth. Scrape down the sides of the bowl and add the salt, thyme, and brandy. Whip again 30 seconds until combined.

Roll in parchment paper or place in a sealed container and refrigerate for up to one week.

Ostrich Sauté Serves 4

You'll find a surprising number of ostrich farms in the Southwest. And why not? Ostrich meat is healthful, flavorful, and fun. You can find ostrich meat online, or ask for it at your local butcher shop. The key to a good ostrich dish is to not overcook it. It's extremely lean, similar to venison, so the more you cook it, the dryer it will become. Use a meat thermometer to make sure it doesn't go past medium rare. In this particular case you don't have to worry too much, though, because it will be swimming in a delicious pan sauce.

2 pounds ostrich steaks, approximately 1½ inches thick

1 tablespoon salt

1 teaspoon pepper

¼ cup blended oil

1 teaspoon minced garlic

1 tablespoon minced shallots

½ cup Red Wine Chile Jelly (recipe follows)

1 cup Veal Stock (page 110)

Season the ostrich with salt and pepper.

Heat the oil in a large sauté pan. Add the ostrich and sear on each side for about 5 minutes until golden brown and cooked to medium rare. If it needs more time, place it in a 350-degree F oven for a few minutes. When it reaches medium rare, remove from the heat and tent with foil to keep warm. Allow to rest 10 minutes.

In the same sauté pan, add the garlic and shallots and cook 1 to 2 minutes until tender. Add the jelly and bring to a simmer; then add the veal stock. Simmer until reduced by a quarter, about 5 minutes.

Ladle the sauce onto a serving plate, and over the sauce place several thin slices of the ostrich. Serve with Creamy Polenta (page 94).

Red Wine Chile Jelly Makes 4 cups

This jelly is great to add to stocks and demi-glace. The acidity in the wine will give sauces a nice finish and the chile adds a surprising spice note.

1 bottle (750 ml) cabernet sauvignon or other dry red wine

1½ cups sugar

½ cup chile powder, lightly toasted

¼ cup liquid pectin

In a large pot, simmer the wine, sugar, chile powder, and pectin. Cook until the sugar is dissolved. Remove from heat and chill until solid. Store in a glass jar in the refrigerator.

✓ Creamy Polenta Serves 4–6

Polenta is a good vehicle to pick up a sauce and take it for a ride, and that's why it's a nice layer for a poultry or meat dish. Change up the cheese if you like—blue cheese or goat cheese will reeducate your palate.

½
2 medium onions, finely diced

1 clove garlic, minced

¼
½ pound butter, plus 2 tablespoons

1¼ cup water

1¼ cup whole milk

¾ cup coarsely ground cornmeal

1 teaspoon salt

½ cup grated Parmesan cheese

In a medium pot over low heat, sauté the onions and garlic in the 2 tablespoons butter until tender. Add the water and milk and bring to a simmer. Slowly add the cornmeal while whisking and bring to a simmer. Simmer for 1 hour while whisking frequently, every 5 to 10 minutes. Remove from heat and stir in the ½ pound butter, salt, and cheese before serving.

Chicken Stock Makes 1 gallon

This chicken stock is meant to be subtle and clean in flavor. Try roasting the bones and vegetables to get a darker color and more developed flavor.

6 pounds chicken bones, necks, and backs

½ pound chicken feet (optional)

1 cup carrots, large dice

1 cup celery, 1-inch slices

1 pound yellow onions, large dice

4 peppercorns

1 bay leaf

1 teaspoon salt

2 quarts ice

Rinse the bones, necks, feet (if used), and backs and remove any organs or excess blood.

Place the chicken pieces, carrots, celery, onions, peppercorns, bay leaf, and salt into an 8-quart stockpot and cover with 4 quarts of cold water.

Slowly bring to a simmer. Once the stock is simmering, add 2 quarts of ice and immediately skim the fat that rises to the top. Bring back to a simmer and cook for 45 minutes, continuing to skim the fat.

After 45 minutes, remove from the heat and let sit for 15 minutes to allow the particles in the stock to settle to the bottom. Remove the stock from the pot by using a ladle to remove the top first. Strain and discard the sediment on the bottom of the pot.

Cool immediately. Freeze for up to 2 months or refrigerate and use within 4 days.

Amish Chicken Cutlets Serves 2

While it's easy to find chicken and other poultry at the grocery store, those plastic-wrapped industrial birds are no comparison to birds raised on pasture of a small, local farm. This is true for any meat, but it's especially the case for chicken. I purchase my chicken from an Amish farm that focuses on free range and natural birds. You can taste the difference.

¼ cup blended oil

4 chicken cutlets (5 ounces each)

1 teaspoon salt

¼ teaspoon pepper

½ cup sun dried tomatoes, lightly packed

¼ cup roasted garlic (page 62)

1 cup chardonnay

1 cup chicken stock (page 95)

½ stick butter

1 tablespoon fresh thyme, chopped

In a sauté pan, heat the oil until shimmering. Season the chicken with the salt and pepper and place in the pan. Cook until browned on one side. Remove the chicken from the pan and set aside. Keep warm.

Add the tomatoes and garlic to the pan, followed by the chardonnay. Boil until reduced by two-thirds. Add the chicken stock and boil until reduced by half. Add the chicken back to the pan and cook for 8 to 10 minutes until done. Remove the cutlets from the pan to a serving plate. Stir the butter and thyme into the sauce. When the butter is melted and incorporated, pour the sauce over the cutlets.

Foie Gras Serves 6

Foie gras is a touchy subject because many people think the production method is cruel. Hudson Valley Foie Gras is the premier *foie gras* supplier in America. Their product is the best and they also employ humane practices in raising their ducks. *Foie gras* is a decadent treat, but please source responsibly.

1 whole lobe of duck *foie gras*, about 1½ pounds, slightly chilled

2 teaspoons salt

1 teaspoon pepper

3 Granny Smith or other tart apples, peeled and sliced

½ cup brown sugar

¼ cup Calvados or other apple brandy

6 brioche halves, lightly toasted

Carefully pull apart the 2 lobes of the *foie gras* with your hands and use a small paring knife to remove the veins between them. Cut each lobe into 1-inch-thick slices. You should have about 6 pieces, 4 ounces each.

Score the top of each piece and season with salt and pepper. Press the salt and pepper into the top side of the liver. Save any leftover bits and use to make *foie gras* butter (page 92).

Heat a medium sauté pan and add the liver, seasoned side down. Cook 30 to 40 seconds on each side until well caramelized. Remove from the pan to rest, keeping covered.

Lower the heat to medium and pour out a bit of the rendered fat, leaving about 2 tablespoons in the pan. Reserve the excess. Add the apples to the pan and sauté for 2 to 3 minutes. Add the brown sugar and cook until the sauce becomes the texture of caramel. Remove the pan from the heat and add the Calvados. Return the pan to the heat and bring to a boil. When it boils, remove from heat and serve immediately.

While the sauce is cooking, spread some of the reserved fat on the brioche. Place a slice of *foie gras* on each piece of toast. Drizzle the sauce and apples over each piece and serve immediately.

Chicken Meatballs in Mole Serves 6

There's more to chicken than just the breast. This recipe shows off the moist goodness of the thighs. It's best to grind them yourself at home, but if you can't, you can always ask your butcher to do it. The blueberries add a nice sweetness to a rich and decadent mole.

Mole

5 ounces tomatillos, husked and rinsed

½ cup sesame seeds

½ cup fresh lard or vegetable oil

3 ounces dried *mulato* chiles

1 ounce dried *pasilla* chiles

2 ounces dried ancho chiles

6 cups hot water

3 cloves garlic

½ cup almonds

½ cup golden raisins

½ teaspoon ground cinnamon

½ teaspoon pepper

Pinch of freshly ground cloves

1½ ounces Mexican chocolate, chopped

1 slice white bread, darkly toasted

2 cups water

2 quarts chicken stock (page 95)

4 teaspoons salt

⅓ cup sugar

Meatballs

2 pounds boneless, skinless chicken thighs, cut into ½-inch pieces, or 2 pounds ground chicken thighs

6 ounces pork fatback, cut into half-inch pieces

7 ounces stale bread, torn into chunks

½ cup loosely packed fresh cilantro, coarsely chopped

2 cloves garlic, chopped

1 teaspoon fennel seed

2 teaspoons ground cumin

1 teaspoon pepper

1 tablespoon coarse salt

¼ cup red wine

½ cup dried blueberries

2 large eggs, beaten

(continued)

Mole: Roast the tomatillos under a very hot broiler until lightly charred, about 5 minutes per side. Remove from the broiler into a bowl and set aside. In a dry sauté pan toast the sesame seeds. Add to the tomatillos.

In a 12-quart soup pot, heat the lard or oil over medium heat. Lightly fry the chiles for 20 to 30 seconds on each side and remove them from the pan. Drain the excess fat from the chiles.

Place the chiles in a heat-proof bowl and cover with 6 cups of hot water. Rehydrate for 30 minutes, then drain, reserving the soaking liquid, and remove the seeds and stems. Puree in a blender with 5 cups of the soaking liquid until smooth.

While the chiles are soaking, fry the garlic and almonds in the same pan until lightly browned. Remove and drain the excess fat from the garlic and almonds, then add them to the tomatillos.

Fry the raisins and stir for 20 to 30 seconds until they've lightly browned. Remove them and add to the tomatillos.

To the tomatillo mixture, add the cinnamon, pepper, cloves, chocolate, and toasted bread. Add 2 cups of water and mix well.

Fry the chile puree over medium heat in the fat until reduced and dark, 20 to 25 minutes.

Puree the tomatillo mixture until smooth and add to the chile sauce. Cook for 15 to 20 minutes, or until reduced by half. Add the chicken stock and bring to a boil. Lower to a simmer and cook for 2 hours. Remove from heat and season with salt, pepper, and sugar to taste. Set aside.

Preheat oven to 375 degrees F.

Meatballs: Grind the chicken into a chilled bowl using a grinder fitted with a coarse plate.

In a large bowl, mix together the fatback, bread, cilantro, garlic, fennel seed, cumin, pepper, and salt. Pass through the grinder and into the bowl with the chicken. Add the wine, blueberries, and eggs, mixing until well combined.

Roll the meatball mixture into golf ball–size balls and place on an oiled roasting rack. Bake until golden brown and cooked through, 20 to 25 minutes. Remove from the oven.

To serve, ladle a serving of mole into each of 6 shallow bowls, and top with the meatballs.

Egg Salad Serves 2

This isn't your typical, boring egg salad. But like any egg salad, the eggs are the star. Look for pastured eggs from a local farm, if you can. They're fresher than grocery store eggs and have those beautiful, dark, sunset-orange yolks. The *sous vide* will do all the work and make sure the eggs are cooked perfectly. I like to plate the eggs with a simple aioli and cornichons, but feel free to mix it up with whatever you like: caramelized onions, black pepper, or sundried tomatoes. And cornichons aren't the only pickle: try pickled carrots, Brussels sprouts, or shallots. However you do it, this will make you look at egg salad in a whole new way. And don't forget to thank the chickens.

6 farm fresh eggs

2 ounces chicken skin

Vegetable oil spray

Pinch of salt

Pinch of pepper

½ cup Garlic Aioli (recipe follows)

1 cup cornichons, sliced

Baby carrots and petite greens for garnish

Set the *sous vide* to 73 degrees C following the machine's instructions. Add the whole eggs to the water and cook one hour.

Meanwhile, preheat the oven to 320 degrees F.

Lay the chicken skin on a cutting board. Clean any excess fat or sinew off and discard. Place the chicken skins in a single layer on a parchment-lined baking sheet. Spray the top with vegetable oil and lightly season with salt and pepper. Cover with another layer of parchment and place another baking sheet on top. Bake for 30 to 40 minutes until the skin is crispy. Remove the top pan and parchment and flip the skin over. Return to the oven uncovered and bake an additional 5 minutes or until golden brown. Remove from the oven and rest on a rack to cool.

Remove the eggs from the water bath and put them in a bowl of ice water to stop the cooking. Drain and remove the shells. Slice them in half lengthwise. This is best served with eggs that are still slightly warm.

To assemble, add ¼ cup of the aioli to each plate. Stack the eggs, cornichons, and crispy chicken skin on top. Garnish with the baby carrots and petite greens and season if needed.

Garlic Aioli Makes 1 cup

Ditch the mayonnaise from the jar. Aioli holds for weeks in the fridge and it's easier to make than you think.

2 medium garlic cloves

1 teaspoon Dijon mustard

1 large egg

½ cup blended oil

½ cup grape seed or vegetable oil

2 teaspoons freshly squeezed lemon juice

⅛ teaspoon salt

Place the garlic, mustard, and egg in the bowl of a food processor. Process until evenly combined, about 10 seconds. With the motor running, slowly add the blended oil in a thin stream and follow with the grape seed oil. Process until completely combined, about 2 minutes. Stop the processor, add the lemon juice, season with salt, and pulse until thoroughly mixed. Stop and scrape down the sides of the bowl with a rubber spatula, then pulse until all the ingredients are evenly incorporated. Remove from the processor bowl and refrigerate.

Fried Chicken Oysters with Black Pepper Tarragon Sauce Serves 2

Remember the excitement of cracking open your piggy bank when you were a kid? This is my adult food version of that same excitement. The chicken oyster is the small pearl of meat on the back near the thigh, and it's a succulent little morsel. I have certain butchers who will save them for me, and I freeze them in my chicken oyster piggy bank. When I have a few dozen saved up (because you can't eat just one), I break the bank and cook up this delectable dish.

Oysters

24 chicken oysters

1 cup buttermilk

2 cups all-purpose flour

1 cup finely ground cornmeal

1 tablespoon salt

2 teaspoons pepper

1 quart canola oil, for frying

Dipping Sauce

1 tablespoon cracked black pepper

2 tablespoons fresh tarragon

¼ cup buttermilk

¼ cup Garlic Aioli (page 102)

2 tablespoons Greek yogurt

4 teaspoons red wine vinegar

¼ cup vegetable oil

1 tablespoon chives, minced

Pinch of salt

Pinch of pepper

Oysters: Add the chicken oysters to the 1 cup of buttermilk and refrigerate overnight. Remove from the refrigerator and strain.

Mix the flour, cornmeal, salt, and pepper together. Toss the oysters in the flour mixture.

In a medium saucepot, heat the oil to 340 degrees F. Add the chicken oysters to the oil 12 at a time. Fry for 6 to 8 minutes until golden brown and cooked through. Remove from the oil and drain, seasoning immediately with salt.

Dipping Sauce: Add the pepper, tarragon, buttermilk, aioli, yogurt, vinegar, vegetable oil, and chives to a blender and puree until smooth. Season to taste with salt and pepper.

To serve, pile the oysters on a plate with a dish of the sauce on the side for dipping.

Stewed Whole Chicken Tortilla Soup Serves 8

This recipe comes from the best chef I know—my mom. When I became a chef, she became educated about new and different foods from those in her usual repertoire. She also felt challenged to create new culinary masterpieces for the family. The reason I love this dish so much is that despite all the new techniques my mom has learned, this soup hasn't changed at all. It's a true Clark family classic.

1 chicken (2½ pounds), roasted

1 quart chicken stock (page 95)

1 quart water

3 cups chopped white onions, divided

2 ribs celery, sliced

1 carrot, sliced

2 ancho chiles

1 *guajillo* chile

3 cloves garlic, smashed

1 tablespoon dried Mexican oregano

2 bay leaves

2 sprigs fresh thyme

1 tablespoon salt

1 teaspoon pepper

¼ cup blended oil

2 cups diced green bell pepper

2 cups cored and diced vine-ripened tomatoes

1½ cups roasted, peeled, and seeded Anaheim chiles

¼ cup roasted garlic (page 62), smashed into a paste

¼ cup fresh-squeezed lime juice

12 red corn tortillas, cut into thin strips and fried until crispy, for garnish

1 cup *queso fresco* (page 106) or grated Monterey jack, for garnish

1 cup green onions, sliced thinly, for garnish

1 cup cilantro leaves, for garnish

4 limes, quartered, for garnish

Place the chicken in an 8-quart stockpot and cover with stock and water. Add 1 cup of chopped onion, celery, carrot, ancho and *guajillo* chiles, garlic, oregano, bay leaves, thyme, salt, and pepper. Bring to a simmer and cook for 1 hour, skimming off any fat or impurities that rise to the top. Remove from heat. Remove the chicken to a baking sheet to cool and strain the remaining broth. If necessary, add cold water to the broth so that it measures 1 full gallon. Set aside.

When the chicken is cool enough to handle, remove the bones and skin and pull all of the meat. Reserve the meat for later.

In a large pot, heat the oil and sauté the remaining onion and the bell pepper until tender, about 5 minutes. Add the tomatoes, roasted chiles, and roasted garlic. Cover with the strained chicken broth and add the reserved meat. Simmer for 15 minutes and skim any impurities or fat that rise to the top. Add the lime juice. Season with salt and pepper if needed.

Serve a healthy portion of soup with the tortilla strips, cheese, onions, cilantro, and limes, as you desire.

Cheeses

When people think of Southwestern cooking, sometimes they're under the mistaken impression that everything is covered in a layer of gooey cheese. If you've been looking through this book, you know nothing is further from the truth. But a really good cheese can add a different dimension to a dish without overwhelming it. Here are a couple of my favorites:

Cotija A cow's milk cheese, this one is aged until it's crumbly and very salty. It doesn't melt very well, but it makes a good garnish for soups, tacos, salads, or about anything else you can imagine.

Dry Jack This is the aged version of that old standby from California, Monterey Jack. When it's aged for 10 to 48 months, it develops a rich, nutty, assertive flavor and a brittle texture, almost like Parmigiano Reggiano. It has a natural rind and a pale yellow color, and it's excellent grated over almost anything. It's also nice just to nibble with some salumi and pickled vegetables.

Queso Fresco (this page) This is a soft, mild, salty cheese that adds a nice contrast, both in appearance and flavor, to roasted vegetables, tacos, soups, black beans, enchiladas, or salads. It's one of my favorite cheeses and it's one you can make in your own kitchen in just a few simple steps.

Queso Fresco Makes 1 pound

Surprise your friends with this believe-it-or-not easy cheese recipe. The fresher the milk, the better the cheese, so buy from a local dairy farm if you can.

1 gallon whole milk

2 cups buttermilk

1 tablespoon citric acid dissolved in ¼ cup warm water, or 1 cup lime juice

2 teaspoons salt

Heat the milk and buttermilk in a large pan. Place a thermometer in the pot and once the temperature reaches 75 degrees F, remove the pan from the heat immediately and cover. Let rest for 3 hours.

After 3 hours, return the pan to medium heat and stir in the citric acid and salt. Place a thermometer in the pot and stir every few minutes until the temperature reaches 195 degrees F. Remove from heat and let rest for 5 minutes.

Strain through cheesecloth. The curd should be trapped in the cheesecloth and the remaining liquid or whey will drain through. Wrap the cheese tightly in the cheesecloth and hang over a bowl for 1 hour in the fridge to expel excess whey. Tightly wrap the cheese in plastic and store in the refrigerator for 4 to 5 days.

Note: For jalapeño-citrus queso fresco, add 1 tablespoon minced jalapeño and grated zest from 1 orange and 1 lemon.

THE OTHER CHICKENS

Center-of-the-plate options seem to be changing rapidly. Gone are the days of 32-ounce porterhouse steaks and monster bowls of chili. That's not a bad thing. We're learning to respect our meats, where they come from, and what they offer. When you source local, grass-fed meats that haven't been treated with antibiotics and hormones or raised in a feedlot, you understand that you don't need to be a glutton. The meat is expensive, but you can balance the plate with more starches and vegetables and still feel like you've had a satisfying meal. Watch the twelve-ounce steak shrink to five. See the braised short rib being stretched out with Arborio rice and sweet peas. It's a return to the old ways of eating, and it's healthful and respectful.

Hanger Steak Chimichurri Serves 4

Everyone likes filet mignon for its tenderness and everyone melts for a fatty, big-flavored rib eye. If you find yourself caught between the two, then give hanger steak a try. Tender and full of flavor, the hanger steak, also known as the butcher's steak, is a prize on its own. The *chimichurri* topping will awaken all of your senses and you won't even need a side dish...unless it's another side of hanger steak.

Chimichurri

1 red onion

1 red bell pepper

1 poblano

1 Anaheim chile

¼ cup chopped parsley

¼ cup chopped cilantro

2 tablespoons fresh lime juice

¼ cup red wine vinegar

1 tablespoon minced garlic

2 tablespoons blended oil

½ teaspoon salt

½ teaspoon pepper

Steaks

4 hanger steaks
(6 to 8 ounces each)

1 teaspoon salt

¼ teaspoon pepper

1 teaspoon smoked sweet paprika

2 tablespoons blended oil

Chimichurri: Heat the grill to medium high.

Slice the red onion into half-inch slices.

Grill the onion slices until tender and roast the bell pepper, poblano, and Anaheim chile until blackened. Remove from the grill and place the peppers in a bowl. Cover with plastic and allow to sit for about 15 minutes. When cool, remove the charred skin, stems, and seeds.

Dice the roasted peppers and onion slices into small pieces.

In a small bowl, combine the diced peppers and onion with the parsley, cilantro, lime juice, vinegar, garlic, and oil. Season to taste with salt and pepper.

Refrigerate for at least two hours or overnight.

Steaks: Preheat the oven to 350 degrees F.

Season the steaks with salt, pepper, and smoked paprika.

Heat a large ovenproof sauté pan over medium heat and add the oil. When the oil shimmers, add the steaks to the pan. Sear each side until browned. Remove from heat and place the pan in the oven for about 8 to 10 minutes to finish cooking to the desired doneness. Remove from the oven, and then remove the steaks to a serving platter and tent with foil to keep warm. Let rest for 10 minutes.

Slice the steak thinly. Serve over a bed of French fries and cover with *chimichurri*.

Lamb Porterhouse with Cascabel Chile Glaze Serves 4–6

For such an unusual cut of lamb, the lamb porterhouse finds its way into a lot of supermarkets. A large part of the filet mignon and the New York strip are separated by a delicious, its-OK-to-pick-up-and-nibble bone. A lamb is smaller than a steer, so unlike a beef porterhouse, the filet on this cut can be rather petite. That's why *sous vide* is the cooking method of choice. By controlling the cooking of both the filet and the New York strip, despite the difference in size, you'll get a perfect medium-rare throughout. Top it off with a glaze of *cascabel* chiles and you're done.

6 lamb porterhouse steaks (5–6 ounces each)

1 teaspoon salt

¼ teaspoon pepper

6 cloves garlic

6 rosemary sprigs

¼ cup herb oil (page 51)

7 *cascabel* chiles

1½ cups hot water

1 cup port wine

1 cup red wine vinegar

1 cup cherry juice

½ cup veal stock (page 110)

1 clove garlic, sliced

Yogurt, for garnish

Place each steak in an individual food-safe bag and sprinkle with ¼ teaspoon salt and a pinch of pepper. Add 1 garlic clove, 1 rosemary sprig, and a tablespoon of herb oil to each bag. Use a food sealer to seal the bags.

Set the *sous vide* temperature to 57.5 degrees C according to the instructions, place the bags of steak in the water bath, and cook for 30 to 40 minutes.

While the lamb is cooking, make the glaze. Add the *cascabel* chiles to hot water and let steep for 10 minutes. Drain, reserving the liquid. Remove the stems from the chiles and then add the chiles and steeping liquid to a large saucepot. Add the port, vinegar, grenadine, veal stock, and garlic. Simmer until reduced by half, 10 to 12 minutes. Remove from heat and allow to cool slightly.

Puree the sauce until smooth and strain through a fine strainer lined with cheesecloth. Set aside and keep warm.

Before the lamb is finished, heat the grill to high.

Remove the bags from the water bath and remove the steaks from the bags. Place on the hot grill for 2 to 3 minutes per side.

Remove from the grill and serve with the sauce and a dollop of yogurt, if desired.

Veal Stock Makes 1 gallon

Veal stock is a welcome addition to red meat braises, rich stews or sauces, and even a morning-after Bloody Mary. Keep a supply in your freezer because powdered stocks and bouillon cubes just aren't the same.

5 pounds veal bones

¼ cup canola oil

1 teaspoon salt

½ teaspoon pepper

¾ cup diced carrots

2 stalks celery, 1-inch slices

1½ cups diced onions

1 cup tomato paste

2 cups red wine

4 peppercorns

1 bay leaf

2 garlic cloves

1 pig foot, halved (optional)

6 quarts cold water

Preheat oven to 375 degrees F.

Rinse the veal bones under cold water. Dry.

Toss the bones in the canola oil and sprinkle with salt and pepper. Place in a roasting pan and roast 1½ hours until golden brown. You may need to strain the fat from the pan as they cook.

Leave about ¼ cup of fat in the pan and add the carrots, celery, and onions.

Smear the tomato paste over the bones so that it creates a thin layer around the surface of the bones. Continue roasting until the tomato paste has browned and the vegetables are caramelized and tender. Remove from the oven.

Add the roasted bones and vegetables to an 8-quart stockpot.

Heat the roasting pan on the stove top and pour in the red wine. Scrape the bottom to remove any caramelized bits. Pour into the stockpot.

Add the peppercorns, bay leaf, garlic cloves, and pig foot to the stockpot and cover with the cold water. Bring to a simmer and cook uncovered for 5 hours. Skim the fat and impurities that rise to the top, every 20 minutes.

Remove from the heat and let sit for 15 minutes to allow the particles in the stock to settle at the bottom. Using a ladle, remove the stock from the top of the pot, leaving the sediment on the bottom to discard. Strain and cool.

Freeze for up to 2 months or refrigerate for use within 4 days.

Cast-Iron Flank Steak with Shrimp Salsa Serves 4

Nothing beats a steak seared in a screaming hot cast-iron pan. A bit of butter at the end will baste and flavor this underrated cut of beef. Thinly sliced and topped with rock shrimp salsa, this steak gives surf-and-turf a new meaning. Rock shrimp not enough shrimp? Add a few jumbo shrimp to the cast-iron and let them bathe in the browned butter. Now we're talking.

Salsa

½ cup minced red onion

½ cup yellow bell pepper, roasted, peeled, seeded, and diced

½ cup poblano, roasted, peeled, seeded, and diced

½ jalapeño, minced

¼ cup cilantro, chopped

1 teaspoon chopped garlic

1 lime, juice and zest

½ teaspoon ground cumin

1 teaspoon paprika

1 teaspoon salt

⅛ teaspoon pepper

Steak

1 flank steak (1½-pound), cut in half across the grain

2 teaspoons salt

½ teaspoon pepper

¼ cup blended oil

2 tablespoons chile-lime butter (page 115)

1 cup rock shrimp, peeled and roughly chopped

Salsa: Combine the onion, bell pepper, poblano, jalapeño, cilantro, garlic, lime juice and zest, cumin, paprika, salt, and pepper. Set aside.

Steak: Season the flank steak with salt and pepper.

Heat a cast-iron pan over high heat. Add the oil and when it shimmers, add the steak. Cook 5 to 6 minutes on the first side, and then flip over and cook an additional 3 to 4 minutes for medium rare. In the last few minutes of cooking, add the butter and rock shrimp to the pan. Spoon the hot butter and shrimp over the steak until the shrimp is cooked through, 2 to 3 minutes. Remove from heat

Remove the steak from the pan and let it rest, covered, for 10 minutes.

Add the rock shrimp to the salsa.

To serve, slice the steak across the grain and spoon the salsa over.

Chorizo Roasted Pork Belly Makes about 8 pounds

Take traditional bacon. Now remove the smokiness and replace it with chorizo spices: hot paprika, cumin, and annatto. Remove the nitrates by using a natural cure with real salt. Wait a few days, and now you can replace that traditional a.m. crispy bacon with a new, spicy treat.

1 pork belly (10–12 pounds), skin on

4 ounces Basic Cure (page 39)

2 teaspoons smoked salt

2 tablespoons chile powder

1 tablespoon ancho chile powder

1 tablespoon hot paprika

1 tablespoon smoked paprika

1 teaspoon ground coriander

1 teaspoon ground annatto

1 tablespoon dried oregano

2 teaspoons cayenne

1 teaspoon pepper

1 tablespoon chopped garlic

Trim the belly so the edges are square.

In a small bowl, mix together the cure, smoked salt, chile powders, hot and smoked paprika, coriander, annatto, oregano, cayenne, pepper, and garlic.

Rub the spice mixture into the belly, coating on all sides. Place the meat into a non-reactive container and refrigerate for 7 days. Each day flip the belly and redistribute the juices and spice mixture evenly around the surface.

After day 7 the belly should be firm. Remove from the refrigerator and rinse thoroughly. Pat dry and let it air dry in the refrigerator, uncovered, overnight.

Preheat the oven to 350 degrees F. Place the belly on a roasting rack and roast 25 to 30 minutes or until the internal temperature reaches 150 degrees F. Remove from the oven and cool.

At this point you can cut the belly into slices, *lardons*, or giant slabs. Refrigerate for up to 2 weeks or freeze for up to 3 months.

Chorizo Sausage Makes 1 pound

This should be a staple for every kitchen in the Southwest. They say bacon makes everything better—in the Southwest, so does fresh chorizo!

1 pound boneless pork butt,
cut into ½-inch pieces, or 1 pound ground pork

2 ounces pork fatback (optional)

1 tablespoon red chile flakes

1 tablespoon chile powder

2 cloves garlic, minced

1 teaspoon salt

½ teaspoon black pepper

¼ teaspoon dried oregano

¼ teaspoon ground cumin

Pinch of ground clove

Pinch of ground coriander

¼ cup white vinegar

1 tablespoon water

If you don't have a meat grinder, in a large bowl mix together the ground pork, fatback (if used), chile flakes, chile powder, garlic, salt, black pepper, oregano, cumin, clove, coriander, vinegar, and water.

If you're going to grind your own, chill the meat grinder. Mix the meat and fatback (if used) with the pepper flakes, chile powder, garlic, salt, pepper, oregano, cumin, clove, coriander, vinegar, and water and place in the freezer for about an hour. The pork should be very chilled but not frozen. Set up the meat grinder with a small plate and immediately grind the pork into a chilled bowl.

Wrap the sausage tightly with plastic wrap and refrigerate overnight before using.

Three Onion Butter
Makes 2 pounds

A chef's secret ingredient for turning out a tender, juicy, flavorful steak is something everybody has in the refrigerator—butter. This special compound butter will make any steak more succulent. Just add a pat to the pan before you sear the steak, and then add a slice to the top of the steak while it takes a rest after cooking.

2 pounds unsalted butter

1 large yellow onion, sliced, grilled, and coarsely chopped

1 large red onion, sliced, grilled, and coarsely chopped

4 scallions, grilled and coarsely chopped

1 teaspoon salt

½ teaspoon pepper

Heat a heavy skillet over medium heat.

Slice 1½ pounds of the butter so that it will melt faster and add it to the pan, whisking frequently. The butter will foam a bit, then subside. Watch carefully as lightly browned specks begin to form at the bottom of the pan. Smell the butter; it should have a nutty aroma. Remove from heat and place on a cool surface to help stop the butter from cooking further and perhaps burning. This requires care, as it's easy to go from browned to burned. Let the butter cool to room temperature.

Whip the browned butter with the reserved ½ pound softened butter. Mix in the onions and scallions and add salt and pepper to taste. Store in a tightly closed container in the refrigerator for up to two weeks or freeze for up to four months.

Compound Butters

Compound butters are simply butter mixed with different aromatic flavorings. They add some zip to everything from roasted corn to your morning toast and can add depth and a little complexity to a sauce. They freeze well, and you'll have something fun and home-made for your next dinner party.

To make compound butter, soften a pound of unsalted butter at room temperature and then mix in the flavorings. Roll it into parchment or put it into a sealed tub and refrigerate or freeze. Here are a couple ideas, but be as creative as you want:

Chili-lime butter Combine 1 teaspoon salt, 1 tablespoon chile powder, and the juice and zest of 1 lime. Mix into the butter and refrigerate or freeze.

Honey Butter Combine 1 teaspoon salt and ½ cup honey with the butter. Mix until well blended, then refrigerate or freeze.

Ancho Braised Lamb Shanks
with Couscous, Greek Yogurt, and Preserved Lemon Serves 4

I'm proud of this recipe because it made the front page of the food section of the *Chicago Tribune*. I cook this all the time, and so should you. It's homey, rich, and comforting, and makes everyone want a seat at the table. I like to serve over Israeli couscous and ladle on the braising jus.

2 tablespoons salt

1 tablespoon freshly cracked black pepper

1 tablespoon ground cumin

4 lamb shanks (16 to 20 ounces each)

¼ cup grape seed oil

1 large white onion, roughly chopped

1 large carrot (or three small), roughly chopped

2 stalks celery, chopped

3 roasted garlic cloves (page 62)

1 cup Malbec or other dry, full-bodied red wine

1 gallon veal stock (page 110) or beef stock

1 bay leaf

6 whole ancho chiles

1 package Israeli couscous

½ cup plain Greek yogurt

2 teaspoons chopped preserved lemons
(page 53)

3 teaspoons freshly snipped mint

1 teaspoon finely minced garlic

2 teaspoons lemon zest

Arugula or radish sprouts

Preheat oven to 325 degrees F.

In a small bowl, stir salt, pepper, and cumin together. Rub the mixture into the lamb shanks.

Heat the grape seed oil in a heavy skillet. Add the lamb shanks and sear on all sides until well browned. Remove from the skillet and set aside.

In the same skillet, sauté the onion, carrot, and celery for 10 minutes until softened and golden brown. Add the garlic cloves and deglaze the pan with the red wine. Add as much stock as will fit in the pan, along with the bay leaf, and bring to a boil.   *(continued)*

Place the lamb shanks in a very large roasting pan. Pour the hot stock and vegetables over the meat. Heat the remaining stock until boiling and add to the roasting pan along with the ancho chiles. Cover the roasting pan tightly with foil and place in the oven for 4 hours.

Remove the pan from the oven and cool shanks and vegetables in braising liquid. Refrigerate overnight.

Before serving, preheat oven to 350 degrees F.

Remove the pan from the refrigerator and skim any congealed fat.

Remove the shanks from the pan. Reheat the braising liquid and strain out the vegetables. In an oven-safe pan over medium heat, reduce the braising liquid by one-third. Add the shanks to the pan and place in the oven. Spoon the braising liquid over the shanks every 5 minutes until the shanks are heated through and glazed with the braising liquid, 25–30 minutes.

While the shanks are reheating, toast the couscous in a hot pan until golden brown. Follow the package directions to boil the couscous. Add salt and pepper to taste.

Mix the yogurt, preserved lemons, mint, and garlic together to make a sauce.

To serve, place a mound of couscous in a shallow bowl and then top with a lamb shank. Spoon braising sauce over all. Garnish with a dollop of Greek yogurt sauce and sprinkle with the finely grated lemon zest and fresh sprouts.

Classic Chili Serves 10

This chili is the foundation—where you take it next is up to you. In the past, I've added cocoa, maple syrup, and dried chipolata sausage. It's your turn to experiment and have fun.

1 beef chuck roast (5 pounds)

2 tablespoons salt

1 teaspoon pepper

½ cup vegetable oil

½ pound onion, diced

½ ounce garlic, chopped

2 cups canned tomato puree

1 quart veal stock (see page 110)

1½ cups diced green chiles,
roasted, peeled, and seeded

2 jalapeños, minced

½ cup chile powder

2 tablespoons hot paprika

5 tablespoons ground cumin

3 tablespoons dried oregano

2 tablespoons chopped cilantro

Cut the roast into small cubes and season with salt and pepper.

Heat the oil in a pot over medium-high heat. Add the beef and brown in small batches. Remove the meat from the pan and add the onion and garlic. Sauté until tender. Return the meat to the pan and add the tomato puree, stock, green chiles, jalapeños, chile powder, paprika, cumin, oregano, and cilantro to the pan and bring to a simmer. Cover the pot and simmer on low for 1 hour. Remove from heat and adjust the seasoning if needed.

Roasted Pork Butt Serves 10

Prepare this one for the big game, or any game for that matter. It goes in the oven the night before and will be ready right before kickoff. We start with a mélange of spices, my not-so-secret blend. The spices penetrate the meat, which becomes fall-off-the-bone tender during the long, slow braise. My classic salsa verde (page 34) bumps up the acidity levels, leaving you with a well-balanced dish.

1 bone-in pork butt (10–13 pounds)

3 tablespoons salt, or as needed

1 cup Not-So-Secret Spice Blend (recipe follows)

1½ quarts chicken stock (page 95) or water

Salsa Verde (page 34)

Heat the oven to 275 degrees F.

Season the pork butt well with salt, then cover it with 1 cup of the spice blend and rub it in.

Place the pork butt in a large roasting pan and add the stock. Cover the pan with foil and place in the oven for 6 to 8 hours. Make sure the foil is sealed so that no steam can escape. This could cause the pork to dry out or burn.

When the pork is cooked, remove from the oven, uncover, and allow to cool enough to handle. Pull the bone from the middle and shred the meat.

Serve with the Salsa Verde and a stack of warm tortillas. You can also use the meat as a taco filling, to stuff chile rellenos, or in pork tamales (page 122).

Not-So-Secret Spice Blend Makes 1½ pounds

This calls for a trip to the local spice shop, and if you don't want to take the time to mix it all yourself, you can ask them to do it. Store it in a large jar with a tight-fitting lid in a dark corner of the pantry, and use it on pork, chicken, vegetables, and even popcorn.

1 ounce ground annatto

½ ounce cayenne

½ ounce powdered celery seed

2 ounces chile powder

⅛ ounce ground cinnamon

1½ ounces ground coriander

½ ounce ground cumin

½ ounce curry powder

1 ounce freshly ground black pepper

1 ounce garlic powder

1 ounce jalapeño powder

1 ounce lemon peel granules

1 ounce orange peel granules

1 ounce Mexican oregano

1 ounce mustard powder

1 ounce onion powder

2 ounces paprika

2 ounces smoked sweet paprika

2 ounces tomato powder

Mix all spices together well.

Mojo Marinade Makes 2 cups

Every chicken should take a swim in this, and so should their pork and fishy brethren.

¾ cup orange juice

6 tablespoons lemon juice

2 tablespoons lime juice

1 tablespoon annatto seeds

1 garlic clove, chopped

1 tablespoon salt

1 teaspoon pepper

½ teaspoon dried oregano

½ teaspoon ground cumin

½ teaspoon cinnamon

2 tablespoons chopped cilantro

¼ cup blended oil

Add the orange juice, lemon juice, lime juice, annatto seeds, garlic, salt, pepper, oregano, cumin, cinnamon, cilantro, and oil to a blender and puree until smooth.

Pour over meat and marinate as necessary.

Marinades

I believe in keeping things simple, but sometimes you might want to add a little extra something to a piece of meat, and that's when marinades come in handy. Skip those bottled things from the grocery store with their preservatives and high-fructose corn syrup and make your own. You can use almost any liquid and a set of aromatic spices to create the flavor profile you have a hankering for. If you want Asian, try some soy sauce with some ginger and garlic. Wine, fruit juices, and even coffee can get you started. Add chile powder, a little cumin and oregano, and your guests will think you're a genius.

Marinades not only add flavor, but they can help tenderize tough cuts. While beef, bison, and sometimes pork can benefit from a long soak, you have to be careful with more delicate meats like chicken and fish. Leaving those in a marinade for too long will actually cause the fibers to break down and the meat will become mushy.

Pork Tamales Serves 10

I make these several dozen at a time and freeze them. Then when I'm hungry, it's a quick fix for a simple dinner.

1½ pounds roasted pork butt (page 119)

1 cup enchilada sauce (recipe follows)

2 dozen dried corn husks

2 tablespoons chile powder

2½ cups *masa harina* (page 89)

1¾ cups veal stock (page 110) or water

½ cup lard or vegetable shortening

½ teaspoon baking soda

1 tablespoon salt

In a skillet, combine the pork and enchilada sauce and heat until warmed through. Set aside.

Soak the corn husks in hot water until pliable.

Whip the chile powder, *masa harina*, veal stock, lard, and baking soda with a mixer until light and fluffy. Stir in salt.

Drain the corn husks.

Place 2 tablespoons of the *masa* mixture on the smooth side of the corn husk and spread evenly through the middle, leaving an inch and a half on all sides. Place 1 tablespoon of the pork mixture lengthwise down the middle of the *masa*. Roll the husk and fold under. Tie the husk with butcher's twine.

Steam the tamales in a large pot seam side down for 40–50 minutes. At this point they can be served with enchilada sauce on the side or cooled and frozen.

Enchilada Sauce Makes 1½ quarts

The great French chef Escoffier left this out of his repertoire of sauces. Don't make the same mistake he did. This is a nice addition to all kinds of Southwestern dishes, from eggs Benedict to burritos and, yes, even enchiladas.

¼ cup blended oil

4 medium *guajillo* chiles, stemmed and seeded

3 cloves garlic

1 can (28-ounce) San Marzano tomatoes

½ teaspoon ground cumin

2 cups chicken stock (page 95)

2 tablespoons lime juice

1 tablespoon sugar

1 tablespoon salt

1 teaspoon pepper

Heat the oil in a skillet and toast the *guajillo* chiles until fragrant. Add the garlic, tomatoes, cumin, and stock and bring to a simmer for 10 minutes. Remove from heat, cool slightly, and puree. Add the lime juice, sugar, salt, and pepper, tasting and adjusting if necessary.

Store in an airtight container in the refrigerator or freeze.

Spice-Rubbed Pork Loin Serves 8–10

When I was in culinary school, I wrote down a select few recipes. When the chef told me, "You better take this one down or you're an idiot," I did. This spice rub comes from one of my mentors who taught me more than any other chef at the Culinary Institute of America. I had to put this one in the cookbook because no matter how great a chef you become, you have to remember it's okay to borrow someone else's recipe once in a while.

½ cup dark brown sugar

½ cup sweet paprika

¼ cup kosher salt

¼ cup chile powder

¼ cup dry mustard

1 tablespoon freshly ground black pepper

2 tablespoons crab boil seasoning, such as Old Bay

½ teaspoon ground ginger

1 bone-in pork loin (12–13 pounds)

Mix together the brown sugar, paprika, salt, chile powder, mustard, pepper, crab seasoning, and ginger.

Place the pork loin on a rack in a large roasting pan. Coat liberally with the spice blend.

Heat the oven to 325 degrees F. Place the loin in the oven and roast to an internal temperature of 140 degrees F, 60 to 70 minutes. Remove from oven and let rest 15 minutes before slicing.

Oxtail Sugo and Mesquite Flour Gnocchi Serves 6

Braised oxtail is the epitome of nose-to-tail eating. You should be able to find oxtail at your local super-market or butcher shop, but you may have to ask for it. Oxtail has tons of flavor, just the right amount of fat, and a tender, meaty texture that melds well with this floral gnocchi. Allow the pillows of crispy dumplings to soak up the sugo and change your thoughts about boring red sauce.

Sugo

5 pounds oxtail, bone-in

1 teaspoon salt

½ teaspoon pepper

¼ cup blended oil

2 large garlic cloves, minced

1 medium onion, diced

½ carrot, diced

⅔ cup dry red wine

3 cups chopped tomatoes, peeled and seeded

1 bay leaf

3 sprigs thyme

2 quarts veal stock (page 110)

Gnocchi

2 pounds baking potatoes

2 egg yolks

¼ cup salt plus 1 teaspoon

4 tablespoons mesquite flour

½ cup all-purpose flour, plus more for dusting

1 gallon water

4 tablespoons unsalted butter

Salt and pepper to taste

Parmigiano-Reggiano cheese, freshly grated, for garnish

(continued)

Sugo: Sprinkle the oxtail with salt and pepper.

Heat the oil over medium heat in a heavy pot just large enough to fit the oxtail. Add the oxtail and fry until golden brown on all sides. Transfer the oxtail to a plate.

Reserve 2 tablespoons of oil in the pot and add the garlic, onion, and carrot. Sauté the vegetables until they start browning. Add the red wine and bring to a boil, scraping all the browned bits off the bottom of the pan. Add the tomatoes, bay leaf, thyme, and stock, and then add the oxtail. Make sure the oxtail is mostly submerged, then cover loosely with a lid. Turn down the heat to low and simmer for about 3 hours or until you can easily stick a fork into the oxtail.

When the oxtail is tender, remove it from the pot and use a fork to shred the meat. Use a spoon to skim off any excess fat (a little is okay, but you don't want an oil slick on top). Add the meat back to the sauce, which should now be pretty thick. If it's watery, turn up the heat a bit and reduce it until thickened.

While the *sugo* is cooking, make the gnocchi.

Gnocchi: Preheat oven to 375 degrees F.

Scrub the potatoes and bake for about 1 hour until tender. Remove from the oven and cool.

When cool enough to handle, split the potatoes in half, scrape the flesh and discard the skins. Run through a food mill or ricer. Measure the potatoes.

Mix 2 cups of the prepared potatoes with the yolks and 1 teaspoon salt. Add the mesquite flour and all-purpose flour. Mix until a dough begins to form. The dough should be smooth and slightly sticky. Add more all-purpose flour if needed.

Flour a work surface and divide the dough into quarters. Roll each quarter into a half-inch-thick rope and then cut the rope into 1-inch pieces. Press the pieces against a gnocchi paddle or fork to form grooves. Place the gnocchi on a floured sheet pan as you work. When all of the dough has been worked, chill the pan in the refrigerator for 15 to 20 minutes.

Place the 1 gallon of water and the ¼ cup of salt in a large stockpot and bring to a boil.

Drop the gnocchi into the water in batches. When they float, usually after 1 to 2 minutes of cooking, transfer them to a baking sheet sprayed lightly with vegetable oil. Once all the gnocchi is cooked, transfer the sheet pan to the refrigerator and chill for at least 20 minutes.

Heat the butter in a large sauté pan. Once the butter is melted, add the gnocchi and let them brown on one side for 3–4 minutes. Flip each gnocchi and lightly season with a sprinkle of salt and pepper. You may have to do this in batches, depending on the size of the pan. Add 4 cups of the sugo to the pan and heat through to finish cooking the gnocchi.

Serve in large pasta bowls with a generous topping of cheese and more sugo, if desired.

Sous Vide Short Ribs
with Smoked Mushroom Anaheim Chile Demi-Glace Serves 4

This is the modern-day version of a slow-cooker dish. Seventy-two hours in a water bath, trapping the flavors deep inside the meat, creates short ribs that will change the way you look at slow cooking. Use bone-in short ribs because the bone adds even more flavor as they cook for a long period of time. It's important to use a good vacuum sealer because there can't be any air in the bags with the meat.

4 short ribs, bone-in (14–16 ounces each)

4 tablespoons beef fat or blended oil

1 cup oyster mushrooms, cleaned, dried, and sliced

½ cup Anaheim chile, seeded, stemmed, and diced

2 tablespoons blended oil

½ cup cabernet or other full-bodied, dry red wine

1½ cups veal stock (page 110) reduced to ⅓ cup

Vacuum seal the ribs individually with 1 tablespoon of beef fat each. Preheat the *sous vide* water bath to 144 degrees F. Add the short ribs and cook for 72 hours.

An hour before the ribs are done, make a smoked mushroom and Anaheim chile *demi-glace*:

Place the mushrooms and chile in a 1-gallon plastic zipper bag. Use The Smoking Gun (page 7) to blow mesquite wood smoke into the bag. Seal the bag for 30 minutes to allow the smoke to infuse the mushrooms and chiles.

Heat a saucepan and add the blended oil. When the oil shimmers, add the smoked mushrooms and chiles. Sauté until the mushrooms have colored and have lost most of their moisture, about 5–6 minutes. Add the red wine and reduce until the pan is dry, about 5 minutes. Add the reduced veal stock and simmer for 5 minutes. Remove from heat and set aside.

Remove the meat from the bags and slice off the bone. Serve with the *demi-glace*.

Rattlesnake Hushpuppies with Orange Pepper Jelly Makes 3 dozen

I saved this one for last so I wouldn't scare you away. Rattlesnake has an amazing and unique flavor. Many Southwesterners call it the desert whitefish. It tastes kind of like chicken, but it has a delicious scent of lake fish. I suggest buying meat instead of a whole snake. The yield of meat to bones is small and it saves you the hassle of skinning and cleaning the snake before you cook it. If the purchased meat is already cooked, then you need only chop it into small pieces. If it's raw or you're cooking the whole snake, place it in a saucepan and cover with water, the juice from half a lemon, and a teaspoon of salt. Simmer it for an hour, then cool, separate the meat from the bones, and chop it.

1 cup yellow cornmeal

1 cup all-purpose flour

3 tablespoons sugar

1 tablespoon kosher salt

1 tablespoon baking powder

1 large egg, lightly beaten

1 cup whole milk

3 tablespoons melted bacon fat or melted butter

12 ounces cooked rattlesnake meat, chilled

Vegetable oil for frying

2 teaspoons salt

Orange Pepper Jelly (recipe follows)

In a large bowl, whisk the cornmeal, flour, sugar, salt, and baking powder. Add the egg, milk, and melted bacon fat and whisk until smooth. Stir in the chilled rattlesnake. Cover and refrigerate the batter for at least 45 minutes.

In a large saucepan, heat 2 inches of oil to 360 degrees F.

Remove the batter from the refrigerator and stir. Drop tablespoon-size balls of batter into the hot oil, about 4 at a time, and fry, turning a few times, until they're deeply browned and cooked through, 3 to 4 minutes. With a slotted spoon, transfer the hushpuppies to a plate lined with paper towels and season with salt immediately. Repeat with the remaining batter.

Serve hot with the Orange Pepper Jelly on the side.

Orange Pepper Jelly Makes 2 cups

It's sweet, it's spicy, and it works well with all kinds of savory breads. The habaneros will add a lot of heat, so if you don't want to feel so much burn, use only one, or even half of one.

**1 red bell pepper,
seeded, stemmed, and finely diced**

**1 yellow bell pepper,
seeded, stemmed, and finely diced**

**1–2 habaneros or to taste,
seeded, stemmed, and minced**

1 tablespoon fresh minced ginger

½ cup cider vinegar

¼ cup fresh orange juice

Zest from 1 orange

½ package (1¾-ounce) dried fruit pectin

2½ cups sugar

Mix the red and yellow bell peppers, habaneros, ginger, vinegar, orange juice and zest, pectin, and sugar in a saucepan and boil over medium heat for 1 minute. Skim any foam that rises to the top. Pour the mixture into a 1-quart glass jar to cool. Stir frequently while cooling to suspend the peppers evenly throughout the jelly.

Store in the refrigerator.

SWEET TOOTH

As a chef, I've always worked in scratch kitchens where there was never a can of pre-made marinara or production-line mayonnaise to be found on the shelves. Not every restaurant in America has a chubby pastry chef in the back of the kitchen who wants you to lick the spoon. Lots of smaller scratch kitchen restaurants don't have the dough to shell out for one guy to bake tarts and whip cream. This forced me to learn my way around spun sugar and tempered chocolate. I look at desserts in a different way than most. For one, I don't like really sweet things. Two, I'm a chef, not a pastry chef. I like to balance sweet, savory, salty, and sour. These sweet bites are all a vision of that balance in the last course. It's time to indulge!

Classic Churros Makes 16 churros (5 inches each)

We're lucky in the Southwest to be surrounded by a great food culture. I learned how to make real churros on one of my trips to Mexico. This recipe is simple and as real as it gets. The churros are crunchy and chewy, and the dipping sauce, with its kick of bourbon, will knock your socks off.

Churros

1 cup sugar

1 teaspoon cinnamon

1 tablespoon ancho chile powder

4 tablespoons vegetable oil

2 tablespoons grated *piloncillo* sugar or brown sugar (see note)

2 cups all-purpose flour

Pinch of salt

2 cups water

1 quart vegetable oil, for frying

Dipping Sauce

6 ounces dark chocolate

2 ounces milk chocolate

2 tablespoons corn syrup

1 cup heavy cream

2 tablespoons Blanton's bourbon (or your favorite)

Churros: In a small bowl, mix together the sugar, cinnamon, and chile powder. Set aside.

In a saucepot, combine the 4 tablespoons of oil, *piloncillo*, flour, and salt with the water. Bring to a boil while whisking. When the mixture begins to thicken, switch to a wooden spoon for stirring. The mixture will form a ball once completely heated through. Remove from the heat and be sure it is all mixed evenly and is smooth.

Heat the vegetable oil in a large saucepot to 365 degrees F.

Put the dough into a *churrera*, a cookie press fitted with a ⅜-inch fluted opening, or a canvas pastry bag fitted with a ⅜-inch star tip. It's important to use canvas because plastic will break. Push the dough out into 5-inch pieces and fry for 6 to 8 minutes, basting with hot oil, until cooked thoroughly. Cook 1 churro at a time; do not overcrowd the pot. Remove from the oil and drain. Toss in the sugar mixture to coat and set aside.

Dipping Sauce: Place the dark chocolate, milk chocolate, corn syrup, and cream into a double boiler and melt, stirring until combined. Remove from heat and stir in the bourbon.

To serve, place the warm churros in a basket and add a bowl of the chocolate dipping sauce on the side.

Note: *Piloncillo* is an unrefined sugar that comes in little pyramids or blocks. You have to grate it to use it, and the flavor is more intense than regular brown sugar. If you can find it, it's worth using, but if you can't, brown sugar will do.

Chocolate Basics

Chocolate is nearly everybody's favorite dessert, and it helps to know just a little about it when you're going to create confections that will have everybody raving.

Bittersweet, semisweet, or dark chocolate
Dark chocolate can't contain any milk solids, and better brands have a higher percentage of cocoa—anywhere from 35 to 70 percent. The higher the percentage, the more pronounced the chocolate flavor. Most people enjoy chocolate in the 55 to 70 percent range. The percentage of sugar usually determines whether a bar is bittersweet or semisweet. A higher sugar percentage means less cocoa.

Chocolate chips These are designed to hold their shape during the baking process, and because they have a different cocoa butter content, they aren't a great replacement for bar chocolate when cooking or baking, unless you're making good old Toll House cookies.

Mexican chocolate It has a high sugar content and is usually flavored with cinnamon. Mexican chocolate comes in tablets that should be grated or chopped before using. The high sugar content makes it gritty, so it's not good to eat by itself, but it makes a sweet and authentic hot chocolate.

Ancho Torte Serves 14

This is an homage to my mentor and friend, Chef Alan Zeman. Unfortunately, I forgot to steal this recipe when I left ¡Fuego!, but over the years I've been able to recreate it pretty well. The rich chocolate ganache is powdered with fruity and spicy ancho chile. It's key to serve this at room temperature. But hide it in the kitchen, because it's going to be hard to eat dinner if you're staring at it from across the table.

20 Oreo cookies, finely ground

½ cup butter, melted

19 ounces dark chocolate, 55%

1¼ pounds plus 2 teaspoons butter, softened at room temperature

1½ cups whole milk

1 cup sugar

3 egg yolks, beaten

1 teaspoon vanilla

Ancho chile powder for garnish

Mix the cookie crumbs and melted butter together until well combined. Press firmly into the bottom and sides of a 12-inch tart pan lined with parchment. Chill.

Melt the chocolate in the top of a double boiler.

While the chocolate is melting, cream the butter. Once the chocolate is melted, add it to the butter, beating on low speed.

In a medium saucepan over low heat, warm the milk and sugar for

5 minutes. When the milk is hot and the sugar is dissolved, remove from heat and whisk about ¼ cup into the beaten egg yolks. When completely blended, add the yolks and milk back into the milk in the pan. Stir in the vanilla.

Add the milk mixture to the chocolate mixture and beat at low speed. Scrape the bowl and mix well.

Pour into the prepared crust and refrigerate 6 hours or overnight.

To serve, remove from the refrigerator and let come to room temperature. Dust the top generously with toasted ancho chile powder.

Mexican Chocolate Chunk Cookies Makes 32 cookies

These are better than what Santa Claus found under the tree. You must eat these while they're warm from the oven, so put the distractions away. You'll need two things: yourself and a glass of milk. That's all.

2 cups all-purpose flour

1 teaspoon baking soda

1 teaspoon baking powder

1 teaspoon salt

½ teaspoon ground cinnamon

½ pound unsalted butter, softened

1 teaspoon vanilla

1 cup brown sugar, lightly packed

2 eggs

7 ounces dark chocolate, cut into ½-inch chunks

5 ounces Mexican chocolate, cut into ½-inch chunks

In a mixing bowl, stir together the flour, baking soda, baking powder, salt, and cinnamon.

In a separate bowl, cream together the butter, vanilla, and sugar until smooth and fluffy. Beat in the eggs 1 at a time. Stir in the dry mixture and mix until combined. Fold in the dark chocolate and Mexican chocolate chunks.

Refrigerate for 45 minutes.

Preheat the oven to 350 degrees F.

Line a baking sheet with parchment or a silicon baking mat. Drop the cookie dough onto the sheet by the heaping tablespoon.

Bake 11 to 13 minutes or until golden brown and cooked through.

Let cool for 15 minutes, if you can.

Rhubarb-Pineapple Crumble Serves 10

Rhubarb is one of my favorite fruits, and you'll always find it on my spring menus. It's super tart, so the trick is balancing the tartness with some sweetness. Every piece of rhubarb can vary in flavor, so you be the judge. Before you pop it in the oven, taste it and make the necessary adjustments. If you can get your hands on some butter pecan ice cream, add a scoop to the crumble while it's still warm and you'll be more than pleased.

¼ cup brown sugar

1 cup rolled oats

¾ cup granola, finely ground

2 tablespoons butter, melted

1½ quarts sliced fresh rhubarb

½ fresh pineapple, diced

1 cup brown sugar

1 vanilla bean

Make the crumble by mixing together the brown sugar, oats, granola, and melted butter. Set aside.

Rub the bottom and sides of a 2-quart baking dish with butter.

Preheat oven to 375 degrees F.

Place the rhubarb, pineapple, and brown sugar in a large saucepot. Scrape the beans from the vanilla pod and add to the pot, reserving the pod for another use. Bring to a boil over high heat. Reduce heat to a simmer and allow to cook for about 20 minutes or until reduced by two-thirds.

Pour into the prepared baking dish and sprinkle the top with crumble. Bake until the crumble is browned, 8 to 10 minutes. Remove from the oven and let cool slightly before serving with a scoop of ice cream.

Note: Add the reserved vanilla pod to 2 cups of sugar and let it sit for 2 weeks to make vanilla-infused sugar.

Habanero Crème Brûlée Makes 8

Almost every dessert menu in America has crème brûlée on it, but none are made with one of the world's hottest peppers. Sweet and heat is the secret. Once you crash through the burnt sugar crust, your taste buds will be surprised by the bite. It's up to you to control the heat in this recipe. Taste the base constantly as it cooks, and once it reaches the right level of heat for you, pull out the habanero!

4 cups heavy cream

1 vanilla bean, split lengthwise

Pinch of salt

1 habanero, scored

8 egg yolks

¾ cup plus
2 tablespoons granulated sugar

1 cup turbinado sugar

In a saucepan, heat the cream with the vanilla bean and salt over moderate heat until it lightly simmers. Remove from heat and add the habanero. Steep 2 to 3 minutes for a bit of spice and 10 minutes for more heat. Mash the habanero to release the oils and give it an extra kick.

Whip the egg yolks and granulated sugar until they become a light pale yellow color. Slowly add the hot cream mixture, stirring gently. Taste. If you would like more heat, steep the habanero longer. If not, strain the custard into a large pitcher.

Let rest 10 minutes. Skim off any foam or bubbles that may remain.

Preheat oven to 350 degrees F.

Fold a kitchen towel to fit into a roasting pan and arrange 8 shallow 5-inch-wide ramekins on it. The towel will keep the ramekins in place. Fill the ramekins nearly to the top with the custard. Carefully move the roasting pan to the center of the oven and pour in enough hot water to reach halfway up the sides of the ramekins. Cover the pan loosely with foil and bake for about 1 hour, or until the custards are firm at the edges, but still a bit loose in the center. Remove from the oven.

Transfer the ramekins to a rack to cool completely. Cover and refrigerate until cold.

Sprinkle the top of each custard with turbinado sugar and use a torch to caramelize the sugar. You can also place them under a broiler for a few minutes until the sugar forms a melted crust.

Serve warm or at room temperature.

Hot Cocoa and Chile Serves 4

I remember the cold wind blowing down the streets of Chicago when I ran across this little hole-in-the-wall place that served only two things: *churros* and hot chocolate. My only disappointment was the size of the serving—it seemed too small. But the chocolate was so rich and thick, the serving size was actually perfect. That's what we have here. So, I warn you—don't fill your mug too full!

1 *guajillo* chile

½ ancho chile

2½ cups whole milk

5 ounces Mexican chocolate, chopped

Pinch of salt

1 tablespoon toasted *pepitas* (page 48)

Soak the chiles in hot water until soft. Drain and remove the seeds and stems.

Add the chiles, milk, chocolate, salt, and *pepitas* to a saucepot and bring to a light simmer. Stir constantly so the milk and chocolate do not burn. Once the chocolate is dissolved, transfer the mixture to a blender. Blend on low speed until frothy.

Serve immediately.

Chocolate Lava Cake Serves 6

There's something about this old-school dessert that never gets tiresome. It's just way too good, and the presentation of a warm, gooey, chocolate center sends tingles up my spine. This recipe is all about the timing and the waiting. You might not be able to time it perfectly like a 5-star restaurant, but as long as the outside is hot and fluffy, and the inside spills out awesomeness, you'll have a success.

Nonstick cooking spray

¼ cup sugar for dusting molds

¾ cup unsalted butter

¾ cup dark chocolate (55%) chunks

1¼ cups powdered sugar

5 egg yolks

3 eggs

1 tablespoon bourbon

¼ cup cake flour, sifted

Preheat oven to 375 degrees F.

Spray 6 aluminum cake tins (4-ounce) or ramekins with nonstick cooking spray. Add some sugar inside each tin and shake it around to coat the inside. Discard any excess.

Melt the butter and chocolate together in a double boiler. When completely melted, whisk in the powdered sugar.

In a separate bowl over a pot of simmering water, beat together the egg yolks and eggs until warmed through. Remove from the heat. Stir in the melted chocolate mixture and bourbon. Using a spatula, fold in the cake flour.

Fill each of the prepared tins three-quarters full with the batter.

Place in the oven and bake until each cake is set around the edges but still a bit liquid in the center, 10 to 12 minutes. Remove from the oven and let sit for 1 minute.

Unmold from the tins onto individual serving plates and serve immediately with Tres Leches Ice Cream (recipe follows).

Tres Leches Ice Cream Serves 6–8

Time to step into the laboratory. Please put on those funny looking goggles and oversized gloves. We're making ice cream! Using powdered dry ice to freeze the ice cream base will not only instantly freeze it but will create a smooth, creamy texture as well. Amaze your guests as the ice cream tingles their palates when they dig in.

1 can (13-ounce) *dulce de leche*

1 can (12-ounce) evaporated milk

1½ cups whole milk

1 slice sourdough bread, crust removed

Pinch of salt

1 pound dry ice

Whip the *dulce de leche*, evaporated milk, whole milk, bread, and salt in a blender until smooth. Strain and pour the mixture into the bowl of a stand mixer fitted with the whisk attachment.

Put on safety goggles and oven mitts, and then wrap the dry ice in a kitchen towel and crush it to a fine powder using a meat mallet.

Turn the mixer to medium-high and slowly sift in the dry ice a little at a time. Adding it too quickly will cause the mixture to boil over. Once you get close to incorporating the entire pound of ice, the milk mixture will completely freeze. Turn the mixer to high and beat until most of the gas has escaped.

When serving, be sure to avoid any large pieces of dry ice that may be left over from the freezing.

Zucchini-Hibiscus Cupcakes Makes 2 dozen

I've never been on any of those cupcake shows and I never will be, but these are yummy. One of the first restaurants I worked in served zucchini bread to every table, and I just happened to make it my dinner almost every night. One day, years later, I thought about those numerous meals of zucchini bread and I decided to create this cupcake recipe. It's better than I remember and a perfect ending to any meal. You should be able to find hibiscus powder and extract in a spice shop or online.

Cupcakes

3 eggs

1⅓ cups sugar

½ cup vegetable oil

½ cup apple cider

1 teaspoon vanilla extract

2¼ cups all-purpose flour

½ cup hibiscus powder

1 teaspoon ground cinnamon

1 teaspoon baking soda

2 teaspoons baking powder

1 teaspoon salt

Pinch of ground cloves

1½ cups grated zucchini

Frosting

½ pound unsalted butter, softened

8 ounces cream cheese, softened

4 cups powdered sugar

2 tablespoons hibiscus powder

1 teaspoon hibiscus extract

Cupcakes: Preheat oven to 350 degrees F.

Line 2 dozen muffin tins with paper muffin cups.

In a large bowl, beat the eggs, sugar, oil, cider, and vanilla until combined.

In a separate bowl, combine the flour, ½ cup hibiscus powder, cinnamon, baking soda, baking powder, salt, and cloves.

Gradually stir the egg mixture into the flour mixture just until combined. Fold in the zucchini.

Fill the prepared tins two-thirds full. Place in the oven and bake for 20 to 25 minutes. Remove from oven and cool for 20 minutes.

Frosting: In a large bowl, beat together the softened butter and cream cheese. Add the powdered sugar a cup at a time, beating well after each addition. Once all the sugar is added, mix in the hibiscus powder and extract.

Ice the cupcakes and store in a tightly covered container.

Mango Flambé Serves 4

Enjoy my rendition of the ever-popular Bananas Foster. Mangoes, caramel sauce, and flambéed tequila—oh yeah! Use ripe mangoes and good tequila, something you would sip on. After the flames go up and the show is over, you might want an after-dinner shot of tequila to say goodnight.

4 large scoops vanilla gelato

½ cup sugar

3 ripe champagne mangoes, peeled and diced

¼ cup butter

¼ cup good tequila

Place a scoop of gelato into each of 4 serving dishes and place back in the freezer.

Add the sugar to a sauté pan and heat to medium high. Allow the sugar to melt and begin to brown. Shake the pan slightly to move the sugar around so that it can caramelize evenly. Do not stir. When the sugar is a dark golden brown throughout, in 8 to 10 minutes, add the mango and butter. Let the mango cook until tender, 1 to 2 minutes.

Remove the pan from the heat and add the tequila. If you're cooking over an open flame, carefully ignite the tequila. If you don't have an open flame, use a long stick lighter to ignite and cook off the alcohol.

Once the flame subsides, remove the gelato from the freezer and pour the sauce over each bowl.

Sources

Blended oil:

Queen Creek Olive Mill
http://queencreekolivemill.com

**Sous vide equipment,
PolyScience The Smoking Gun:**

Chef Essentials Restaurant Equipment & Supplies
www.chefessentials.com

Curing salt:

Butcher & Packer
www.butcher-packer.com

**Spices, rattlesnake beans, black rice,
dried chiles:**

Mount Hope Wholesale
www.mounthopewholesale.com

Game meats:

D'Artagnan
www.dartagnan.com

Sonoran white wheat:

Hayden Flour Mills
www.haydenflourmills.com

Prickly pear juice, agave nectar:

Cheri's Desert Harvest
www.cherisdesertharvest.com

Southwestern honey:

Holly's Little Farm
www.hollyslittlefarm.com

Tepary beans, Saguaro seeds, chiltepín:

Tohono O'odham Community Action
www.tocaonline.org

Native Seeds/SEARCH
www.nativeseeds.org

Southwestern vegetables:

Sleeping Frog Farms
www.sleepingfrogfarms.com

Pecans:

Green Valley Pecan Company
www.greenvalleypecan.com

Southwestern grass-fed beef:

Double Check Ranch
www.doublecheckranch.com

American Grassfed Association
www.americangrassfed.org

**Tapioca maltrodextrin,
agar-agar, xanthan gum:**

Willpowder
www.willpowder.net

Seafood:

CleanFish
www.cleanfish.com

Monterey Bay Aquarium Seafood Watch
www.montereybayaquarium.org/cr/seafoodwatch.
aspx

Up-to-date food scenes in the Southwest:

Edible Baja Arizona
www.ediblebajaarizona.com

Edible Phoenix
www.ediblephoenix.com

Slow Food Southern Arizona
www.slowfoodsouthernaz.org

Acknowledgments

Many thanks to my editors, Aaron Downey and Marilyn Noble, who put this book together and oversaw all aspects of the project with great patience and virtue; my sous chef and best friend, Brandon Dillon, who ultimately helped coordinate my life during this busy time; Valerie Vinyard for constantly correcting my grammar; mentors, Alan Zeman, Albert Hall, Andrew Ruga, Elizabeth Mikesell, and Ellen Fenster, who have helped guide me and undoubtedly motivated me; my culinary staff, who inspire me every day to become a better cook through their hard work and determination; my family, for their continued support in my career; and friends, who have heard me out on every little detail. And most important, thanks to the Culinary Institute of America and its world-renowned staff, for providing the best education possible.

Index